Published by Fleming H. Revell, a division of Baker Book House Company
P.O. Box 6287, Grand Rapids, MI 49516-6287
www.bakerbooks.com

Previously published in 1987 under the title
Growing Up Born Again: A Whimsical Look at the Blessings and Tribulations of Growing Up Born Again

Printed in the United States of America

Library of Congress Cataloging-in-Publication Data
Just as we were : a nostalgic look at growing up born again / written by Patricia Klein . . . [et al].
    p. cm.
  ISBN 0-8007-5839-0 (pbk.)
  1. Christianity—Humor. I. Klein, Patricia.
PN6231.C35 J87 2003
230'.002'07—dc21
                                2002014964

Scripture is taken from the King James Version of the Bible.
Cover and interior design: Left Coast Design, Portland, Oregon.

✳ Permissions & Acknowledgments ✳

God's Smuggler comic cover art by Al Hartley is copyright © 1974 by Spire Christian Comics. Used by permission.

The Cross and the Switchblade comic cover art by Al Hartley is © 1975 by Spire Christian Comics. Used by permission.

"Into My Heart" by Harry D. Clarke is copyright © 1924. Renewed 1952 by Hope Publishing Company, Carol Stream, IL 60188. All rights reserved. Used by permission.

"Sermon in Shoes" is copyright © Ruth Harms Calkin, Pomona, CA 91768. Used by permission.

"Turn Your Eyes Upon Jesus" by Helen Howarth Lemmel is copyright © 1922 by Singspiration Music/ASCAP. Renewed 1950. All rights reserved. Used by permission of the Benson Company, Inc., Nashville, Tennessee.

"So Send I You" by E. Margaret Clarkson is copyright © 1954 by Singspiration Music/ASCAP. Renewed 1982. All rights reserved. Used by permission of the Benson Company, Inc., Nashville, Tennessee.

The chart on "God's Dealings With Man in the Plan of Ages" is used by permission of Moody Bible Institute of Chicago.

The illustration of the Rainbow Bible on page 27 is reproduced with the permission of the publisher, World Bible Publishers, Inc.

Illustrations on pages 38, 49, and 133 by Dan Pegoda

The illustrations on pages 13, 150, 160, and 180 are Copyright by the Review and Herald Publishing Association. Used by permission.

The illustrations on pages 28, 61, 81, and 169 are reprinted by permission of the Incorporated Trustees of the Gospel Workers Society, Union Gospel Press, P.O. Box 6059, Cleveland, Ohio 44101.

The illustrations on pages 150 are Copyright Providence Lithograph Company, Providence, Rhode Island. Used by permission.

Very special thanks to the following people for their help:
All friends and family who opened scrapbooks and scoured attics for photographs and relics, including Evelyn Bence, Jane Campbell, Carolyn Corse, Ken and Katherine Corse, Alice Davidson, Jack and Camilla Luckey, T. N. Mohan, Sylvia Rawdon, and Steve Schaefer. Carolyn Corse for her stories, her laughter, and her unfailing enthusiasm. Ken and Catherine Corse, T. N. Mohan, Sylvia Rawdon, and Steve Schaefer for their time and effort in unearthing relics and photographs. Norman Campbell for his creative ideas and contributions. Betty Lukens, Inc., Rohnert Park, California, for their generous permission to use selected pieces of flannelgraph art to illustrate this book.

Every attempt has been made to credit the sources of copyrighted material used in this book. If any such acknowledgment has been inadvertently omitted or miscredited, receipt of such information will be appreciated.

Dedicated, with loving gratitude, to our moms and dads:

Bob and Sue, Jim and Floss, Al and Margaret
Doug and Sue, Alton and Pauline

Contents

If You're Saved and You Know It

What every Christian wants to know about unquestionably sinful and semi-approved activities.

Faith of Our Fathers

Keep your Sunday School attendance streak going, hear inspiring testimonies of prayer meetings and missionary conferences, and celebrate at the potluck fellowship with Jell-O and hot dish of your choice (tuna noodle casserole, anyone?).

The Church's One Foundation

Communion Sunday, baptism, avoiding the world, charting the end times, and other things born-againers do best.

There's Within My Heart a Melody

Are there lingering signs you grew up born again? Take this Semifinal Judgment quiz!

*Introduction

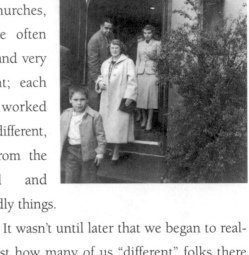

"What's your religion?" Not an unusual question when we were kids. But if you grew up born again, you never knew quite what to say. To reply simply "Christian" or "Protestant" was too vague and to respond with the name of a denomination meant that you put your trust in the wrong things. But the correct answer, "I'm saved" (or "I have received Jesus Christ as my personal Savior"), was often met by blank stares.

charge of everything. We belonged to local churches, which were often very small and very independent; each church worked hard to be different, set apart from the world and ungodly things.

If you were born again, you didn't enjoy the easy identification offered by churches with worldwide memberships, a common liturgy, and one guy in

It wasn't until later that we began to realize just how many of us "different" folks there are. And how we are all different in many of the same ways. The joys of this realization are especially sweet. After all, each of us may have assumed for far too long that we were one of a very few . . . a few who could still hold their own in a sword drill. Who were distressed because no one was teaching the little kids the order of the books of the Bible. Who thought of flannelgraph stories when freshly laundered socks stuck to a flannel nightgown. Whose piano repertoire con-

sisted solely of Sunday School choruses and hymns. Whose mental image of Africa was punctuated by the tiny light bulbs on a missionary map.

With the recognition comes laughter. Not the laughter of ridicule, but the bubbling laughter of affection. *Just As We Were* celebrates our shared experiences and our own personal memories of family life, church life, our nurturing in the faith. Born again folks older than us will remember the same experiences, perhaps from a slightly different perspective.

Christ is the Head of this house, and the unseen Guest at every meal.

Those younger may also recognize their own childhood, though some of the rules seem to change as technology infiltrates our lives. And those from other traditions altogether may begin to understand what it is that makes us different.

As we explore our shared experiences in these pages, we have pulled aside the forms and rituals to discover an essential vitality of belief. Our faith lives. And because it lives, we celebrate. We can laugh at our peculiarities, acknowledge our failings, and gratefully appreciate why we are the way we are. We invite you to share and enjoy along with us.

Chapter One

The Family of God

In order to really understand a born again person, you can't simply visit one of our churches, although we'd love to have you visit our church some Sunday. (How about next week? We can get the church bus to stop by and pick you up.)

Studying our theology won't give you the real picture either. Anyway, most of us would tell you flat out that we don't believe a theology; we believe the Bible.

To really understand a born again person, you have to see us in our natural habitat: in our homes, with our families.

The Family of God

Come on, Mom, Come on, Dad, It's time . . . to pray.
* * *

Every week the radio voice beckoned, and every week families everywhere stopped to pray. Those ten simple words reflect the absolute center of born again life: the family.

Members of a born again family are "peculiar people." The Bible says so, but you knew it anyway. Maybe you didn't realize it right away, but as you grew you began to observe the many ways in which you and your family were just a bit different from your neighbors.

* The Born Again Father *

Your father is different from most of your friends' fathers.

Born again fathers are the heads of their homes, and they take their headship seriously. They are responsible to God for loving their wives as Christ loved the Church (no easy task), and for training up their children in the way they should go so that when they are old they will not depart from it (also not a snap). The born again father leads his family by setting an

10

example, in word and deed, in all areas of life, including Sabbath-keeping, family altar, and discipline.

✴ Dads and Sundays ✴

Unlike your friends' fathers, your father doesn't go fishing on Sundays. Nor does he lounge around in a smoking jacket, chewing on his pipe, while leisurely leafing through the Sunday paper. He doesn't show up at neighborhood picnics with two six-packs of cold beer. He doesn't swear at the dog. He doesn't tell jokes that make the women blush and the men guffaw and slap one another on the back. He

also doesn't mow his lawn or Simonize his car on Sundays.

Born again fathers remember the Sabbath day to keep it holy. Sunday is the Lord's Day, and worshiping God is the main event. It is not a day for pursuing one's own pleasures. The born again father does not *send* his family to Sunday School—he takes them there himself!

✳ Dads and the Family Altar ✳

The born again father's duties as head of the house do not end with Sabbath-keeping. He's responsible for his children's spiritual instruction throughout the week as well. Family altar—a time of Scripture reading and prayer—is held daily. In your home, it takes place in the living room after supper.

Dad reads aloud from the Bible, paraphrasing as needed for the younger children. Sometimes he quizzes the family after the lesson to make sure everyone paid attention. No sweat. You're still young enough that *God* or *Jesus* is the right answer to any question you're asked.

Dad then invites everyone to share prayer requests. You hold your breath. Here's where the evening can get long. Your brother might bring up his need to buy Smitty's old Chevy to drive to school. Your older sister might entreat grace so as not to die of humiliation for being the only girl in school who can't date till she's sixteen. Dad might spend half an hour telling his captive audience about some problem at work. The older children might then jump in with advice. Tensions can escalate quickly from there. Meanwhile, Susan, your best friend from up the block, waits patiently on your front stoop for you to come out and play.

✳ Dads and Discipline ✳

The born again father is most certainly in charge of family discipline. He's head of the house and he's not running a democracy. The family does not sit around and vote on what the rules should be or how to enforce them. Dad's word is law.

Punishments are usually applied to one's backside. No time is wasted in Freudian gropings for the hidden meaning behind the misbehavior. The meaning is obvious: "The heart is deceitful above all things, and desperately wicked: who can know it?" (Jer. 17:9) and "Foolishness is bound in

sending you to your room. Major infractions elicit the dread pronouncement, "Wait till your father gets home."

Sometimes the most effective punishments do not involve spankings. Like the time you stole money from your mother's purse to buy a coffee cake. Mom detects the rustling of the waxy white bakery wrapper under your jacket. "Where did you get the money for this?" she asks. You tell her. The rest of the day you're miserable, dreading what will happen when Dad gets home.

As soon as he arrives, Mom and Dad confer in the kitchen. After supper, Dad announces, "For

the heart of a child; but the rod of correction shall drive it far from him" (Prov. 22:15).

Most often, Mother is the one to discover your acts of disobedience. She handles minor infractions of the rules with scolding, mouth washings, or by dessert, we'll all have a piece of the raspberry coffee cake your youngest sister bought with the money she *stole* from Mother's purse." Everyone stares at you in horror. You stare at your plate. You try to choke down a forkful of the flaky pastry, but it tastes like cardboard and sticks to the roof of your mouth. The moment dinner is over and everyone's excused, you flee to your room and throw yourself, sobbing, across the bed. Dad follows you into your room and sits on the end of your bed, an open Bible in his hand. You expect a spanking. You *want* a spanking to release the guilt that's heavy within you. Instead, your father reads a verse that you will never forget. "Bread of deceit is sweet to a man; but afterwards his mouth shall be filled with gravel" (Prov. 20:17). You learn your lesson.

✶ The Born Again Mother ✶

Mothers of born again families are also "peculiar" in the eyes of the world. Born again mothers look like mothers—not like older sisters. And they only wear makeup when they go to church or to a missionary banquet. (Some wear none at all . . . *ever!*)

You love to watch Mom put on her makeup. First, she lightly dusts her face with powder. Then she puts on her lipstick—a bright red that makes her eyes sparkle and her black hair shine. You wish she'd leave her lips that way. But no. Mother folds a Kleenex in half and blots carefully till only the faintest tinge of pink remains. You sigh. Even without the crimson lips, no one is more beautiful than your mother.

Mother wears clip earrings—never danglies or pierced—and a choker to match. She also wears a little hat. In winter, her coat has a fur collar attachment that looks like a fox biting his tail. The only jewelry on Mother's hands is her wristwatch and her wedding rings. She wears no nail polish, of course. And the seams of her stockings are precisely straight.

Mrs. Gordon down the street is not at all like your mother. She doesn't blot her lipstick. She puts it on thick, like the movie stars in the fifty-cent picture frames at Woolworths. She even outlines her lips to make them look thicker than they really are. She's very thin and wears slacks. She leaves lip prints on her cigarettes (she smokes!) and she does not act or look like your mother at all.

A born again mother is in the kitchen when you get home from school. She's not out playing tennis at some country club. She has an "afternoon surprise" ready for you—a piece of chocolate cake and a glass of milk, or Cracker Jacks from the store. If fathers are the authority figures in Christian homes, representing God the Father, mothers are like the Holy Spirit—the source of love and comfort. It's Mom who Band-Aids your scraped knees, pulls Danny off you when he's beating you up in a fight, dries your tears when your parakeet dies, and holds your hand at the doctor's office.

Born again mothers are very good at being mothers. They are fruitful vines. "Children are a heritage of the Lord: and the fruit of the womb is his

reward. As arrows are in the hand of a mighty man; so are children of the youth. Happy is the man that hath his quiver full of them" (Ps. 127:3–5). Your father thinks birth control is a communist plot. While the Christianized Western world contains its population growth, heathen and communist nations spawn geometrically, eventually overwhelming us through numbers alone. This accounts for all your brothers and sisters. Mom and Dad are not slackers when it comes to safeguarding democracy in the free world.

If You Want to Break a Born Again Mother's Heart...

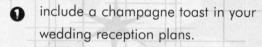

1. include a champagne toast in your wedding reception plans.

2. tell her that you are considering having your baby baptized.

3. forget to hide the liqueur collection in the bedroom closet before she comes over for dinner.

4. become a charismatic.

5. convert to _____.

6. marry a Catholic, Jew, Presbyterian, Episcopalian, or charismatic.

7. admit that you can't remember the books of the Bible in the correct order.

8. show up at a church supper with spinach-and-feta-cheese quiche, croissants, or chocolate amaretto mousse.

✴ The Born Again Home ✴

The born again family's home is different from the homes of the neighbors. There are no ash-trays in a born again home. Stale cigarette smoke doesn't hang in the air, and the carpeting and furniture are not scarred by cigarette burns. No wet bars in the family room. No whiskey decanters, wine racks, or beer steins. No lewd statuettes or ceramic novelties line the windowsills. Nor is the coffee table buried under a mountain of *True Confessions*.

You will find a print of Sallman's *Head of Christ*

over every fireplace mantel, and the bookshelves flanking the fireplace are lined with Christian biographies, Bible dictionaries, commentaries, and fifteen years' worth of *National Geographic.* The magazines on the coffee tables are *Moody Monthly, Decision,* and a host of publications from mission organizations.

The extensive record collection features the *Grand Canyon Suite* and a ten-album set of *50 Classical Favorites* played by the London Symphony Orchestra. There are also Christmas albums (Mitch Miller), George Beverly Shea ("How Great Thou Art"), the Blackwood Brothers, and the Melody Four Quartet.

A large bulletin board spans one wall of a born again family's breakfast nook, and every inch of it is plastered with missionary prayer cards.

Above all, the born again home is comfortable and func-

tional rather than luxurious and grand. Don't look for phones in the bathrooms or carpeting in the basement. Even if you did have that kind of money to throw around, you'd be giving it to missions.

Do You Live in a Born Again House?

The following are items that belong in a born again house. Use the guidelines at the end of the quiz, on page 22, to determine your score.

ART

_____ Scripture verse plaques, 5 points each.

_____ Inspirational poem wall hanging, 3 points each.

Bonus:

_____ If you have a copy of "Footprints" displayed, add 10 points extra.

_____ Any print depicting Jesus, 5 points each.

Bonus:

_____ A print of Sallman's Head of Christ, add 2 points extra.

_____ A print of Jesus in the Garden, add 2 points extra.

_____ A paint-by-number painting or needlework of Jesus, add 15 points extra.

TOOLS

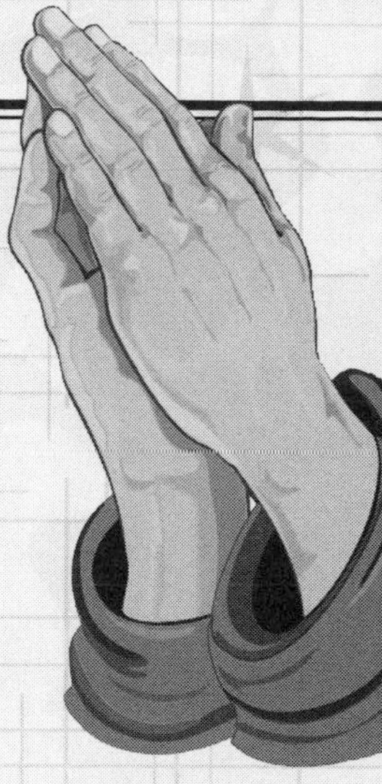

___ A plaster-of-Paris plaque of "Praying Hands," 10 points each.

___ Each Bible in the house, 20 points.

Bonus:

    ___ For each King James Version, add 5 points extra.

    ___ For each Scofield Bible, add 10 points extra.

___ Each missionary prayer card *displayed*, 3 points.

___ Each devotional book, 5 points.

UTENSILS

___ Salt and pepper shakers that have "Ye are the salt of the world" printed on them, 5 points each.

___ Each ashtray *displayed*, subtract 5 points.

___ A Daily Promise Box on the breakfast table, 10 points.

Bonus:

    ___ If it plays "Standing on the Promises" when the lid is opened, add 5 points extra.

SEASONAL DECOR

___ If you erect a large, illuminated Santa Claus and his reindeer on your roof at Christmas, *subtract* 50 points.

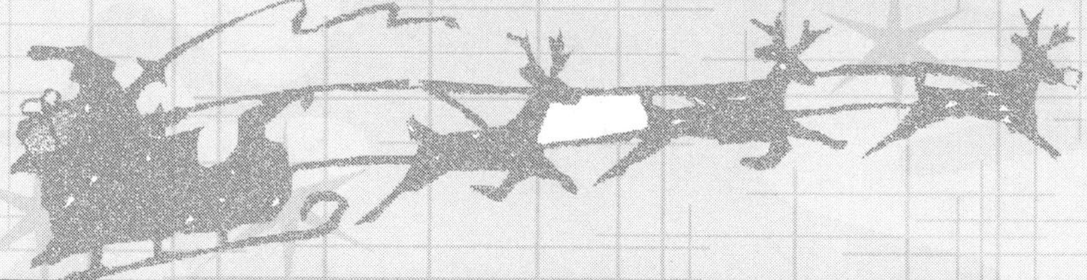

"Bible-Lovers"
Precious Promises
—150—
PRECIOUS PROMISES
FROM GOD'S WORD TO
BRIGHTEN YOUR DAILY LIFE

BOOKS

____ Each Bible reference book, 10 points.

____ Each Danny Orlis or Sugar Creek Gang book, 5 points.

____ Each Christian biography, 3 points.

____ Each Christian pop psychology book, 2 points.

____ Each Christian romance novel, 5 points.

MAGAZINE SUBSCRIPTIONS

____ *Moody*, 10 points.

____ *Decision*, 10 points.

____ *Christianity Today*, 5 points.

____ *Christian Herald*, 5 points.

____ Any mission magazine, 5 points.

____ *Charisma*, subtract 10 points.

(Are you sure you're taking the right survey?)

____ *The Wittenburg Door*, subtract 10 points.

MUSIC

____ Any album by George Beverly Shea, Bill Pearce, or Moody Chorale, 5 points.

____ Any album by Amy Grant, Sandi Patti, or the Gaithers, 3 points.

____ Any album by Stryper, subtract 5 points.

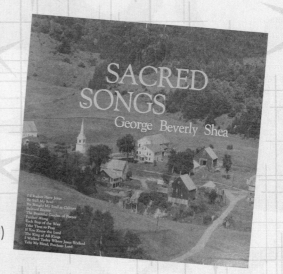

SACRED SONGS
George Beverly Shea

SCORING:

200 points or more: You are, without doubt, a Good Testimony. In fact, you could be called a Great Testimony. Treat yourself to a week at Word of Life Camp this summer.

150-199 points: You are a fine example of a Real Christian. Perhaps you could work just a little on some of your weaker points for next time.

100-149 points: Indicates considerable lukewarm-ness. You are in a serious pre-backslidden condition. Beware!

50-99 points: Perhaps you should rededicate your life.

1-49 points: Have you ever heard of the Four Spiritual Laws?

✳ Other Telltale Signs ✳

The differences go on and on. On Saturday mornings, while your friends head *en masse* to the matinee at the local theater, you ride your bike to Junior Choir practice or play scales at your music teacher's house. Every born again child learns to play an instrument so that he can someday be of service to the Lord by accompanying hymns or playing offertories. Acceptable instruments to study are: piano, flute, accordion, and violin. Doubtful instruments: drums, tuba, saxophone, and electric bass guitar.

You belong to either Pioneer Girls or Boys' Brigade, not Girl Scouts or Boy Scouts. That means different uniforms on different days and different stories to exchange about outings and jamborees.

Born again children have tender consciences and will go to great lengths to avoid telling a lie. One device is to cross your fingers. Whatever you say when your fingers are crossed doesn't count. The trick is to be very careful not to cross two things at the same time. For example, don't cross your fingers if your legs are crossed. This is a double cross and cancels out the first cross. However, if you cross your fingers, your legs, *and* your wrists, the cross counts again. Soon theological problems develop: Do your hairs being crossed count? If so, can you ever know if the total number of crossed hairs is odd or even? Only God can know for sure. He knows the number of hairs on your head and He knows if they're crossed or not.

How do born again parents measure the success of their parenting? This can usually be quantified by how many children are now on the mission field, in pulpits, or in full-time Christian work. Did they attend Christian colleges or Bible schools? Are they married and raising born again families of their own? Are they still different?

Amazing Grace, How Sweet the Sound

The first and great commandment is: There is no excuse for not saying grace three times a day—before breakfast, lunch (sometimes called dinner), and supper (often called dinner). This means you, and this means even in restaurants.

This is a sign of a real Christian. If two people walk into a restaurant and just start shoveling their food down as soon as it arrives, you know that they aren't saved. If, when their food arrives, they both bow their heads and silently say grace, they're Christians but they're not dedicated; they're not bold enough in their witness. But if they both bow their heads and then one of them (the man if it's a couple) audibly says grace, they're your kind of people. You are so sure of this that you might walk up to these perfect strangers and say, "You're Christians?" They'd smile, say yes, and then ask what church you go to. You'd answer and repeat their question. The conversation might end there or continue for several minutes if you

Children's Prayers

TABLE	God is great and God is good; We will thank Him for this food. By his hand we all are fed; Give us, Lord, our daily bread. Amen.
MORNING	Dear Father in heaven, I thank thee for watching over me during the night. Help me to be loving and helpful all day long. Amen.
EVENING	Now I lay me down to sleep, I pray Thee, Lord, my soul to keep; If I should die before I wake, I pray Thee, Lord, my soul to take. Amen.

quickly establish that you know someone who knows a friend of theirs.

Children and new Christians are allowed to memorize standard graces that they can then repeat at every meal. Your mother tells you that the first sentence you ever spoke was "God is great." You quickly followed with "God is good. Let us thank Him for our food." But when you eat at your friend's house you're surprised to hear her say, "Thank You for the world so sweet. Thank You for the food we eat. Thank You for the birds that sing. Thank You, God, for everything."

One day you feel that it's time to put away childish things. Your father asks you to say grace and you take a leap of faith (this has nothing to do with Kierkegaard) and attempt to make up your own prayer. You know the phrases; it must just be a matter of putting them in one order today, another order tomorrow. You leap. "At eventide we give Thee thanks for this Thy bounteous blessing. Bless this food to our use. Bless the hands that have prepared it. Amen." There. You said it, but you're embarrassed because it doesn't sound as good as when Dad says it and because you know everyone else is staring at you. They were expecting you to say "God is great."

Next time you'll really surprise them. Last summer at camp you heard a great prayer. It startled you but the evangelist himself said it, so it must be okay. You can't wait to try it on your family, but the timing has to be right. You know you'll get only one chance to repeat it in front of your parents: "Rub a dub dub, thanks for the grub. Yea, God."

Thank You Prayer

Dear God,

We bow our heads and pray,

Thank You for our food today.

Amen.

The B·I·B·L·E

The B·I·B·L·E

There is no person or book on earth with more authority than the Bible. It is God's Word: holy, inspired, inerrant, and infallible. What does that mean? It means that it's always right! As a born again child, you learn that in order to know God, you need to know the Bible. You need to know how to use a Bible: know *all* the books, in the right order; how to find a chapter and verse; how to pronounce the funny words; how to use the concordance and cross-references. It is no small achievement for a child to learn his way around a Bible!

The version you use is very important. The King James Version is the *real* Bible. Rumors abound that the apostle Paul used the King James Version. ("If it's good enough for Paul, then it's good enough for me.")

WE BELIEVE The BIBLE

You may laugh, but it no doubt would have been his Bible of choice. The King James Version uses the language that God understands. Great words like *thee, thou, begat, woe, hearken.* Verbs ending in *th* or *st: cometh, sitteth, saith, talketh, wast, sleepest.* Imaginative words like *forasmuch, whosoever, mammon, fared sumptuously, thrice, abomination.* Wonderful, mysterious mouthfuls of words.

These are God's words and these are the words we use when we speak to Him. A special holy vocabulary.

Oh, sure, there are other translations, like the Revised Standard Version (used by liberals) and the Catholic Bible (which your parents say includes books of spurious origin). There are a few that are really only paraphrases. These may be okay for devotional reading, but not for really studying the Bible. To really study the Bible, you need to use the real Bible—the KJV.

Teach me faith and duty!

Bible Fun Facts

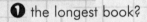

(Knowledge of the Following Fun Facts Does Not Contribute to Your Spirituality.)

Do you know where in the Bible to find . . .

1. the longest book?
2. the longest chapter?
3. the longest verse?
4. the longest word?
5. the shortest book?
6. the shortest chapter?
7. the shortest verse?
8. the shortest verse in the Old Testament?
9. the middle verse?

Answers: 1 Psalms; 2 Psalm 119; 3 Esther 8:9; 4 Isaiah 8:3; 5 2 John; 6 Psalm 117; 7 John 11:35; 8 1 Chronicles 1:25; 9 Psalm 118:8

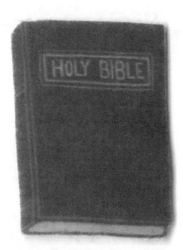

✳ Holy Bible, Book Divine ✳

✳ The Right Bible ✳

As you grow into young adulthood, you begin to notice that the adults' Bibles look different from the kids' Bibles. They are likely to be bigger . . . and, somehow, more spiritual looking.

When you're a kid, your Bible might be white, bright red, or, if you're really fortunate, wrapped in a multicolored scene of Jesus blessing the children, with color plates including Daniel in the lions' den, Jesus entering Jerusalem, and other exciting action pictures. The adults' Bibles, on the other hand, are likely to be a more somber color, maybe maroon, probably black, with maps in the back, but certainly no pictures.

The type is different, too—smaller. And you begin to discover that there is more than just Bible text on these adult Bible pages. There are long introductions to every book, and columns of tiny words and letters running up and down the sides of each page, and blocks of information nestled at the bottom (that sometimes take up nearly half the page).

These notes, you learn, are not Holy Spirit–inspired, as the rest of the Bible is, although they are sometimes quoted with something akin to reverence. It all makes up the New Scofield Reference Bible—described on the title page as featuring "introductions, annotations, subject chain references, and such word changes in the text as will help the reader." These word changes are not done covertly, but slipped

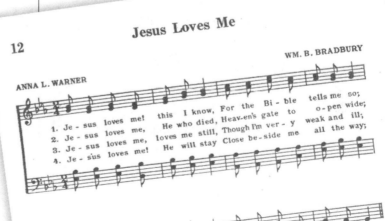

between slender vertical lines to let you know the inspired King James words have been altered. (C. I. Scofield, as everyone knows, has never been guilty of adding to the Holy Writ, as we are warned about in Revelation 22:18.)

You may decide that you want to enter the spiritual big leagues and that you'd like a Scofield Bible of your very own. (Your parents, of course, are more than eager to bestow such a gift.) And once you actually have this handsome, leather-bound volume in your possession, the first thing you need to do is unstick all the pages and underline all the familiar passages in either ink or red pencil. This marks the new Bible as your own, and shows your friends that you are indeed familiar with all the right passages in the Holy Book, that you have spent hours reading and meditating on them in your daily devotions. (It goes without saying that no two pages of your oft-used Bible would ever be left stuck together!) You're the owner of a Scofield Bible and an altogether spiritual person.

*My hope is built on nothing less
Than Scofield's notes and Moody Press . . .*
—Traditional

Thy Word Have I Hid in My Heart

✳ Do You Know All the Words by Heart? ✳

The ability to memorize is crucial to the development and well-being of every born again child. Although you aren't required to memorize prayers or creeds, you need to memorize virtually everything else.

You need to memorize music. For example, you should learn all the words to the choruses that you sing in Sunday School. Like "Rolled Away" with all the hand motions, and all seven verses (plus any you can make up) of "I Have the Joy, Joy, Joy, Joy, Down in

My Heart." Eventually, you will want to memorize the words and tunes to the hymns you sing. It brings a very real sense of satisfaction to be able to sing a hymn in church without looking at the hymnal.

You will also find it helpful to memorize a testimony or two. The old standby "Jesus saves, keeps, and satisfies" is a bit amateurish. So take a little time and memorize your own moving version of being rescued from sin.

A high priority is knowing the books of the Bible by heart. It is not enough to simply know them; you must be able to rattle them off quickly. The current record for reciting all sixty-six books in order is 6.78 seconds. The point of this is not simply to show off, although a great deal of pride does accompany this accomplishment. The

The Books of the Bible

Old Testament

GENESIS · EXODUS · LEVITICUS · NUMBERS · DEUTERONOMY · JOSHUA · JUDGES · RUTH · I SAMUEL · II SAMUEL · I KINGS · II KINGS · I CHRONICLES · II CHRONICLES · EZRA · NEHEMIAH · ESTHER · JOB · THE PSALMS · PROVERBS · ECCLESIASTES · SONG OF SOLOMON

LAW   HISTORY   POETRY

MAJOR   PROPHETS   MINOR

ISAIAH · JEREMIAH · LAMENTATIONS · EZEKIEL · DANIEL · HOSEA · JOEL · AMOS · OBADIAH · JONAH · MICAH · NAHUM · HABAKKUK · ZEPHANIAH · HAGGAI · ZECHARIAH · MALACHI

New Testament

MATTHEW · MARK · LUKE · JOHN · THE ACTS · ROMANS · I CORINTHIANS · II CORINTHIANS · GALATIANS · EPHESIANS · PHILIPPIANS · COLOSSIANS · I THESSALONIANS · II THESSALONIANS · I TIMOTHY · II TIMOTHY · TITUS · PHILEMON · HEBREWS · JAMES · I PETER · II PETER · I JOHN · II JOHN · III JOHN · JUDE · REVELATION

HISTORY   EPISTLES   GEN. EPISTLES

IDENTIFICATION CARD
This Bible is the property of

NAME

STREET

CITY   STATE

If lost, please return to above. Thank you.

purpose of knowing these books in their proper order is that it prepares you to know your way around your Bible. It is the first step in knowing your Bible backwards and forwards.

But most important of all is memorizing Bible verses. Children are encouraged to commit vast quantities of Scripture to memory. There is almost no limit to what a teacher will say or do to get a kid to memorize verses. You have a new memory verse every Sunday, which is to be learned before you get to class. Once in Sunday School, the class repeats the verse several times in unison, and then you try to do it solo. Often you can win prizes, depending on what you memorize. For example, memorizing the Beatitudes plus fifteen other verses could win you a Sugar Creek Gang book. Memorizing the Ten Commandments, Psalm 23, Psalm 100, and the books of the Bible could win you a new white zipper Bible. Memorizing Hebrews 11, 1 Corinthians 13, plus all of the above could win you a week at camp.

When you tire of memorizing, or complain of boredom, longing to do something more stimulating such as play Bible Baseball, you are solemnly warned that your ability to memorize will decline as you grow older. Therefore, you must memorize as many Bible verses as possible while you are still young. Oddly enough, you find this warning very motivating; the adults you know do seem to suffer from some sort of memory decline.

First and Second Hezekiah

Which of these sayings are genuine Bible quotes?

1 Haste makes waste.

2 There is no new thing under the sun.

3 To every thing there is a season.

4 An eye for an eye and a tooth for a tooth.

5 Cleanliness is next to godliness.

6 Money is the root of all evil.

7 Out of the mouths of babes.

8 Today is the first day of the rest of your life.

9 Am I my brother's keeper?

10 The borrower is servant to the lender.

11 Let it be.

12 God helps those who help themselves.

13 A watched pot never boileth.

14 A little child shall lead them.

15 Because you're mine, I walk the line.

Answers: 2 Ecclesiastes 1:9 **3** Ecclesiastes 3:4 **4** Matthew 5:38 **7** Psalm 8:2 **9** Genesis 4:9 **10** Proverbs 22:7 **14** Isaiah 11:6

A Memorization Strategy

A Good Memorization Program Requires Strategy:

❶ Always start with John 3:16. Not only do you know it already (since you've heard it all your life), but it gives you a strategic edge. Your teacher is now conditioned to accept anything else you might repeat. Romans 3:23 and Romans 6:23 are almost as good.

❷ Psalm 23 is good for six quick verses. It gives you momentum, gets the old juices flowing. Beware of verses 2 and 3; if you find yourself lying down in still waters, you're in trouble.

❸ Then throw in some quickies. First Thessalonians 5 has several goodies: "Rejoice evermore," "Pray without ceasing," "Quench not the Spirit." It is recommended that you avoid the one about greeting one another with a "holy kiss." Teachers generally don't appreciate the joke.

❹ Now you can throw in John 11:35, the shortest verse in the Bible, "Jesus wept." It is important not to repeat this verse first, lest your teacher think you are making a mockery of Scripture memorization.

❺ By now, you've memorized ten verses, enough to win something. If you really want to dazzle them, try some verses from 1 Chronicles: "Adam, Seth, Enosh" (1:1) and "Eber, Peleg, Reu" (1:25). To top it all off you can throw in 1 Chronicles 26:18: "At Parbar westward, four at the causeway, and two at Parbar."

On God's Word I'll Stand

✳ The Sword Drill ✳

"All right, children, get out your *swords*," says the kind, starchy lady at the front of the room. "It's time for our sword drill."

She calls Bibles *swords* because "the word of God is quick, and powerful, and sharper than any two-edged sword" (Hebrews 4:12).

You scoot to the edge of your chair, grasping your own sword tightly, your eyes fixed on Mrs. Metcalfe's face.

"Draw swords."

Thirty pairs of hands clutching Bibles shoot into the air.

"First Corinthians 13:13."

"First Corinthians 13:13," bleat thirty young voices after her.

Mrs. Metcalfe's eyes scan the room. She smiles at the trembling anticipation. "Charge."

It's amazing how that thin India paper doesn't tear as young fingers fly past whole books of the Bible—Acts, Romans, Corinthians, here we are. What chapter did she say? Eleven, twelve. . . .

"And now abideth . . . !" shouts the goody-two-shoes in the front row who has jumped to her feet. Everyone else groans, but Mrs. Metcalfe is beaming. "Julia."

Julia straightens up and reads in a calmer voice. "And now abideth faith, hope, charity, these three; but the greatest of these is charity."

"Very good, Julia. You may sit down. Are we ready for the next one? Quiet, please, children. Jeremiah 33:3."

"Charge."

This time you have a head start, because you know that Jeremiah comes after Isaiah and they both come soon after Psalms. You leap to your feet in triumph.

"Call unto me!"

Mrs. Metcalfe nods pleasantly in your direction. "Go ahead, please."

"Call unto me, and I will answer thee, and shew thee great and mighty things, which thou knowest not." It's hard to keep the singsong of triumph out of your voice.

The next verse is Habakkuk 2:4, at which all the boys groan. But it's a simple one to find, really, when you consider that Habakkuk is only part of a foursome: Jonah, Micah, Nahum, Habakkuk. Flipping backwards from the end of the Old Testament, you're bound to run across one of those four almost immediately, and then it's just a matter of nailing down the right one.

Unfortunately, Julia seems to employ the same

technique—or a quicker one, since she's on her feet again in the front row.

"And his brightness."

"And his brightness?" repeats Mrs. Metcalfe.

"Behold, his soul!" you shout.

Julia looks down in confusion at her Bible as Mrs. Metcalfe gives you the nod to continue.

"Behold, his soul which is lifted up is not upright in him: but the just shall live by his faith."

Ha! Julia had Habakkuk 3:4.

And then it begins all over again, the wild ripping through the pages of the Holy Book. The primary reward in excelling at the sword drill is the satisfaction of hearing the teacher call your name and knowing that you beat out the other kids in the room; the way you get to stand and read the Bible verse for all to hear; and the proud, happy knowledge that you are part of a Sunday School elite: the biblically literate.

Genesis, Exodus, Leviticus . . .

Even if there were no such thing as a sword drill, you would still want to have the names of the sixty-six books of the Bible hidden in your heart. And not just the names, but also the right sequence. Your Bible's table of contents is there to help non-Christians find what they're looking for and get saved, but real Christians should never need to use it.

When you grow up you discover that some marketing genius has started selling tabs imprinted with the names of each book. You look around your Sunday School room and see Bibles that have these tabs sticking out, top to bottom, front to back, so that it looks like a school notebook run wild. Even though you're grown up now and you can see what a practical idea this is, the child in you is disgusted. They're crutches. Everyone should have to memorize the books as you did.

You learned a song that goes, "Genesis, Exodus, Leviticus, Numbers, Deuteronomy. . . ." It kind of reminds you of the A, B, C song, but this one is so much longer you think it's never going to end. You're grateful to the person who thought of this song because otherwise the memorization process would be unbearable.

You also study a chart that divides the books up into categories: Law, History, Poetry, Major Prophets, Minor Prophets, Gospels, Acts, Epistles of Paul, Epistles of Other Guys, Revelation. These divisions make the long litany seem not as long.

Once you get them all down—permanently written on your heart—you can find even Hosea without hesitating. What's better, you won't be fooled when someone tries to tell you that there's a book called Hezekiah.

Born Again Lingo

* * *

Red Letter Edition: A Bible that features the words of Christ in red ink. Considered *de rigueur* in certain circles.

Sword Drill: A contest in which children hold their Bibles aloft and, at the word *Charge*, fly through their Bibles trying to be the first to locate and read aloud the verse given by the teacher. Traces of this activity may still be seen in adults who, for example, scurry to be the first to find the texts the pastor is using in his sermon.

Thumb Index: Rounded thumb notches on the edge of a Bible with tabs that indicate the names of the books. Bibles featuring thumb indexes are not permitted in sword drills.

The Word: The Bible. Short for "The Word of God."

Heroes of the Bible Quiz

* * *

This small quiz is designed to test your knowledge of Bible heroes. Any born again Christian worthy of his baptismal certificate ought to know all of the answers. We're making it especially easy for you by asking the questions in rhyme.

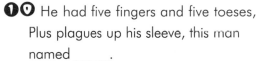

The B+I+B+L+E

❶ This prophet pulled a great big bonah,
He ran from God—his name was _____.

❷ He didn't fear tiger, lion, or spaniel,
This young prophet's name was _____.

❸ His brother took him for a ride on
a seesaw, And this big hairy guy
was _____.

❹ A queen that Haman should not
pester, A real Jewish princess whose
name was _____.

❺ As a partner of Andy he later became
famous, This minor prophet's name was
_____.

❻ As a doctor he was no fluke,
He wrote a Gospel, the man named _____.

❼ As a king of Israel he really stood tall,
Until he blew it—a man called _____.

❽ The serpent's word she did believe,
A really bad break for a lady named _____.

❾ A very pretty and loyal youth,
Naomi's daughter-in-law was _____.

❶❶ He had five fingers and five toeses,
Plus plagues up his sleeve, this man
named _____.

*If you missed any of these, you need to make a quick visit to the nearest Sunday School!
What were you doing all those years? Perhaps it's time to buckle down and start reviewing old quarterlies.*

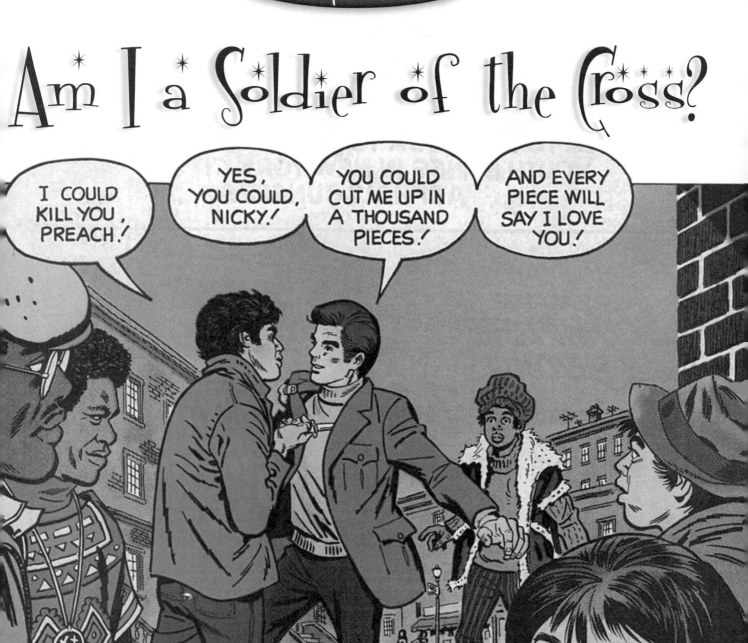

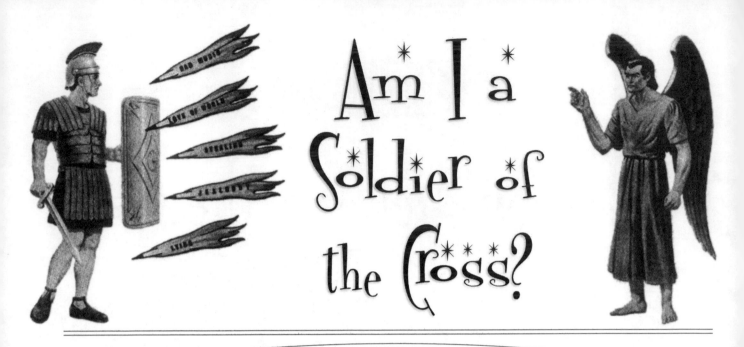

Am I a Soldier of the Cross?

The following inventory has been compiled to help you discover (or rediscover) your own personal born again quotient. Take your time, reflect carefully, and remember, no fair praying!

❶ The pastor announces a love offering. You:
  A. turn to the person next to you and kiss him on the lips.
  B. write a note of appreciation for the evening's speaker and hand it to the usher.
  C. check your billfold for two fives instead of the crisp ten-dollar bill you usually put in the offering plate.

❷ You are at a covered dish supper, sitting next to the missionary who brought the authentic native dish, "banana sardine soufflé." You learn ✳ that masticated bananas form the base of this exotic dessert. Your response is to:
  A. empty your mouthful into your paper napkin.
  B. finish what's on your plate but politely decline seconds.
  C. ask for the recipe.

3 How many angels can dance on the head of a pin?

A. It depends. What kind of dancing?

B. Which order of angels?

C. Isn't this a Catholic problem?

4 A sword drill  is:

A. an instrument of torture used during the Inquisition.

B. a cadet exercise at West Point.

C. a contest to see who can look up Bible verses fastest.

D. what a dentist uses before he says, "Rinse and spit."

5 You have "arrived" as an evangelical when . . .

A. you've visited the Holy Land.

B. you've been baptized in the Jordan River.

C. you've seen the grotto where Jesus was born and decried the commercialism.

D. you've visited the Billy Graham Center at Wheaton College.

E. you've visited anything in Wheaton, Illinois.

6 How many animals of each kind did Moses take onto the ark?

A. Two of most; seven of some.

B. It wasn't Moses—it was Noah.

C. Moses *had* an ark, but he didn't get on it!

7 You see a bumper sticker with this symbol on it. You immediately know that:

A. the driver is a sport fisherman.

B. the driver is a Greek sport fisherman.

C. the driver is a born again Christian.

D. the driver is a fish.

8 When asked what your "life verse" is, you reply:

A. "Huh?"

B. "Well, er, heavens, there are so many good ones, you know."

C. "How do I love thee? Let me count the ways."

D. "Philippians 4:13: 'I can do all things through Christ which strengtheneth me.'"

9 For the past nine years, you've had perfect attendance at Sunday School. Your family is camping out and there is no church nearby. To win the coveted pin for the tenth year running, you:

A. make your parents drive you fifty miles to the nearest Sunday School.

B. beg your parents to hold Sunday School and church under a shade tree, but wonder if it counts since you're all wearing bathing suits.

C. cross your fingers behind your back and say, "Yes," when your Sunday School teacher asks you if you attended Sunday School while on vacation.

10 You're driving to church at breakneck speed so you won't be late. A flashing red light appears in your rearview mirror. What do you do?

A. Pull over and order everyone in the car to pray.

B. Make a break for it down a side street.

C. Turn to your wife and say, "Quick, dear— do that thing you do where you swell up and look pregnant."

11 When you hear the expression "the Fall," you immediately think of:

A. autumn.

B. Rome's decline.

C. man's depravity.

D. Lady Godiva's hairpiece.

12 Finish this sentence: "And all the people said . . ."

A. amen!

B. how lovely the choir looked in their new robes.

C. hubba, hubba!

13 Mom overslept and didn't start the roast before leaving for church. The family should:

A. go to a nice restaurant for dinner.

B. refuse to eat in a restaurant on Sunday since that would signal approval of working on the Lord's Day.

C. compromise by going to a fast food restaurant.

D. This is a trick question; born again moms never oversleep.

14 You know you've been called to the mission field when:

   A. you sample a box of chocolate-covered ants and don't throw up.

   B. you cry while reading *Mary Slessor, White Queen of the Cannibals.*

   C. you can't sleep at night for thinking about the lost souls who have never heard the Gospel.

   D. the guy you have a crush on goes forward at a missionary call.

   E. you reach age twenty and you still aren't married.

15 Which denominational founder is mentioned in the Bible?

   A. John Wesley.

   B. John the Baptist.

   C. Martin Luther.

16 You generously contribute to YFC because you have a deep concern for:

   A. Yiddish factory clerks.

   B. euthanasia.

   C. euthenafrica.

   D. euth everywhere.

17 Who would you most expect to see at the Sunday evening service?

   A. The Mamas and the Papas.

   B. Sister Sledge.

   C. Moody Men's Glee Club.

   D. The Moody Blues.

18 Noah's Ark is:

   A. a chain of pet stores.

   B. described in Genesis 6.

   C. a welding term.

   D. the name of a new singles' bar.

19 You would welcome to your pulpit as a guest speaker:

A. Dr. Erwin Moon.

B. The Reverend Sun Myung Moon.

C. Moon Mullins.

D. The man in the moon.

20 The born again teenager completes "the look" with which black leather objects?

A. Gold-embossed King James Bible.

B. Jacket with skull and crossbones emblazoned across the back.

C. Driving gloves.

D. Miniskirt and go-go boots.

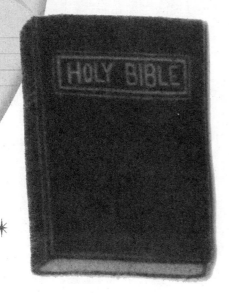

21 Four cars with dashboard accessories arrive simultaneously at an intersection. The born again Christian's car is the one with:

A. the fluffy dice.

B. the plastic statue of Saint Christopher.

C. the compass inscribed with Psalm 103:12.

D. the lady's red garter.

22 It's your turn at the buffet tables at the covered dish supper. You:

A. load up on whatever your mom brought because it's your favorite casserole and she never makes it at home.

B. avoid the green Jell-Os. You can't be sure which ones are made with mayonnaise instead of whipped cream.

C. avoid black mushroom slivers—they could be anchovies.

23 Which TV shows might a Christian watch on Sundays?

   A. "The Ed Sullivan Show."

   B. "What's My Line?"

   C. "Candid Camera."

   D. None of the above.

24 According to the church bulletin, your favorite Moody Science film will be shown during the evening service. You can't wait to see:

   A. *Lord of the Flies.*

   B. *City of the Bees.*

   C. *Planet of the Apes.*

   D. *The Birds.*

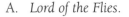

25 Four friends order dinner at a restaurant. You spot the born again Christian when the waitress hands him a:

   A. Cold Duck.

   B. Blue Nun.

   C. Christian Brothers.

   D. Dr Pepper.

26 Which of the following is *not* an animal mentioned in the Bible?

   A. A lion David caught by his beard.

   B. Balaam's ass.

   C. The widow's mite.

   D. Jonah's big fish.

27 Which group would you be least surprised to see in heaven?

   A. The Brothers Four.

   B. The Twelve Disciples.

   C. The Dave Clark Five.

   D. The Chicago Seven.

28 Identify the born again saint from the following list:

A. Saint Nick.

B. Saint Bernard.

C. Saint Louis.

D. Nate Saint.

How Did I Do?

This is something that only you can answer. Taking an inventory like this should be a very personal matter. Moreover, we aren't really concerned in knowing what your answers are. We're not here to judge you. We don't want to make you feel guilty or uncomfortable or out of place. But if you do, perhaps it's time for a little reflection. Why don't you bow your head and close your eyes right now, and pause to consider these matters? Don't worry about the people sitting next to you or your friends. They'll wait for you. And then afterwards, we'll all sing a closing hymn.

I do what I am told

I work quietly

I rest quietly

I finish my work

I keep our room

Chapter Four

If You're Saved and You Know It

*S*aved. *Born again. Redeemed. Converted.* Those of us who grew up in born again families knew that we belonged to a very select body of people. We were special, set apart, chosen. We were real Christians. Of course, there were a lot of people who said they were Christians, meaning they weren't Hindu or Muslim or Jewish. But we knew we were real Christians.

How did we know? Here are some guidelines.

If You're Saved and You Know It

I Would Be Like Jesus: How to Identify a Real Christian

❶ Have You Accepted Jesus as Your Personal Savior?

Your second birth—it doesn't happen when you are born into a Christian family. Nor does it happen when you're dedicated to the Lord as an infant, when you're dunked into the warm waters of the baptistry after Sunday evening service, or when you join the church.

You can't earn salvation by reading your Bible or memorizing verses—not even by leading a good life. And it's not left to luck ("I'll take my chances

Which Road Will Your Boy or Girl Choose?

CHRISTIAN · SECULAR · SPIRITUAL · WORLDLINESS · ACADEMIC · "ISMS" · VOCATION · EVOLUTION · BRIGHT FUTURE · EDUCATION

along with everybody else on the planet"). In fact, there's nothing chancy about salvation at all ("I *might* be born again; I'm not sure; I guess I'll find out when I die"). You either are or you aren't, and if you are, you *know* you are.

Much like natural birth, being born again is a historical event. It takes place at a specific time and in a real location. For example, you may have been born again on June 5, 1958, at summer camp with your counselor after cabin devotions. Or on October 11, 1953, at home with Mother. It's helpful to write this information on the flyleaf of your Bible.

> *God said it.*
> *I believe it.*
> *That settles it.*

If you've accepted Jesus as your personal Savior you know that, unlike your first birth experience (nobody asks to be born!), your second birth was a totally voluntary act of your own will. One day, some time after reaching the Age of Accountability—which is generally thought to be at

Into My Heart

Into my heart,
Into my heart,
Come into my heart,
Lord Jesus;
Come in today,
Come in to stay,
Come into my heart,
Lord Jesus.

—Harry D. Clarke

least five or six years of age and is often marked by an awakened consciousness of nakedness (the very young are totally unself-conscious in the unclothed state, as were Adam and Eve in the garden before the Fall)—you realize that you are a sinner. You sin (small s—steal money from your mother's purse at the first clanging of the Good Humor man's bell in your neighborhood, lie to the teacher about forgetting your homework, beat up your little brother for tattling about the stolen money) because your heart is black with Sin (big S—that streak in your nature that makes looking out for Number One your primary concern in life). You also know that God is holy, "the wages of sin is death," and you are doomed to die.

> *Happy Birthday to you,*
> *Only one will not do,*
> *Take Christ as your Savior,*
> *And then you'll have two.*
> *—Traditional*

Then, happily, you hear the Good News that Christ died in your place! You eagerly accept Christ's sacrifice for you and are very thankful. Usually, you do this with an adult who leads you in the Sinner's Prayer. "Dear Jesus," you pray, "I know I'm a sinner. Please forgive my sins. Thank You for dying on the cross for me. Come into my heart. Amen."

Just As I Am

Just as I am, without one plea,
But that Thy blood was shed for me,
And that Thou bidd'st me come to Thee,
O Lamb of God, I come! I come!
—Charlotte Elliott

Christ died for everyone, it is true. So why isn't everyone saved? You know the answer. To be saved you must personally admit that *you* are a sinner and that Jesus' death is *your* only hope to go to Heaven and not Hell when *you* die.

Growing up born again doesn't just happen. It starts when you answer yes to the question, "Have you accepted Jesus as your personal Savior?"

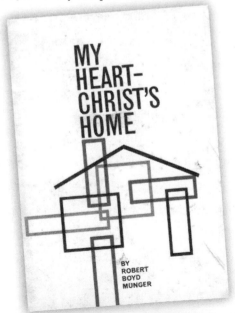

❷ Do You Believe in the Holy Bible?

For a real Christian, the Bible is the primary source of spiritual authority. Whether you call it the Bible, the Holy Bible, God's Word, Holy Scripture, or the Book, it is God's message to His people, both saved and lost. The Bible is inspired, inerrant, and infallible. You should read it daily, meditate on it, study it thoroughly, and commit it to memory. It serves as the source of wisdom and learning, and it is the final authority on all matters temporal and eternal.

❸ Have You Been Baptized?

Make no mistake here. This is believer's baptism, by immersion only. Baptism is the public demonstration of a personal decision, the decision to be saved. It is perfectly obvious that infants can't make such decisions, so infant baptism is out of the question. And since immersion was the way Jesus was baptized, it is the only way to be baptized.

❹ Do You Have Daily Devotions?

If there is one activity that sets you apart as a spiritual person, it is the habit of daily devotions. In the first place, it has been drummed into you for as long as you can remember that having daily devotions is the

Christian thing to do. It enhances your spiritual well-being and helps you get to know God better; it's as vital and regular an activity as brushing your teeth.

In addition, daily devotions is an activity expected of any young person who has truly accepted Christ as Lord and Savior and who earnestly desires to grow in the Christian walk.

For this reason, it's important that people *know* you have daily devotions— which knowledge is not difficult to impart. "Why, just this morning during my daily devotions . . ." is a typical opener. (Morning, not evening, is *the* time slot for daily devotions. "Rising up a great while before day, [Jesus] went out . . . and there prayed," says Mark 1:35.)

Commencing daily devotions is not difficult, either. You have done it countless times. You resolve to spend half an hour every morning between 6:45 and 7:15 propped up in bed reading informative passages in your Bible, writing down exciting discoveries in your notebook, and going down your prayer list interceding for unsaved school friends and the lost of the world.

Only trouble is, your plan usually fizzles after a few days or weeks. The passages in your Bible (especially when you insist on beginning in Genesis) turn out to be something less than riveting. Few "discoveries" seem exciting enough to write down in your notebook. And about the time you reach your second or third prayer request, your attention is diverted by a speck on the opposite wall, or a dust bunny under the dresser, or you remember there's a spelling test today. The half hour drags. Your pillow behind you feels so soft. And it's a little more difficult the next morning—and the morning after that—to rouse yourself early and be "spiritual."

"You get something out of it even when you don't realize it." So says your Pioneer Girls guide. And so, in an effort to do what you're supposed to do, you return to the regimen again and again, despite how much you have or have not gotten out of daily devotions. Even when zealous high school youth group leaders up the ante to an hour, you make New Year's resolutions and vows before God, all in a tireless effort to reach the benchmark of spirituality, the exercise of daily devotions.

⑤ Do You Witness?

Real Christians share their faith. You want everyone to hear the Good News, to have an abundant life, to go to Heaven.

So you tell your friends at school. You pass out tracts at shopping centers. You invite your neighbors to Sunday School. You are part of an evangelistic team that goes to the Skid Row mission every week. You pray for the unsaved. You worry about the people you know (and those you don't) who are headed straight for Hell.

Sermon in Shoes

Do you know, O Christian,
You're a sermon in shoes?
Do you know, O Christian,
You're a sermon in shoes?
Jesus calls upon you
to spread the Gospel news,
So walk it and talk it,
You're a sermon in shoes.
—Ruth H. Calkin

And above all, you are a good testimony. You show by the way you live that you are different, that you have something special about you. Something that helps you through the bad times. Something that gives you a particular joy in living. And when someone asks you about your faith or remarks on your wonderful disposition, you are always prepared to share.

"how can I really *know* the Bible and learn to win souls?"

Amen: Literally, "So be it." Indicates agreement and is often used to punctuate a sermon or statement. While many churches are loud and enthusiastic amen-ers, others are more restrained and dignified. We recommend that you observe carefully before contributing your own heartfelt "Amen." Note: It is always appropriate to reply "Amen" if the speaker says "And all the people said. . . ."

Blessed My Heart: Translation is "I enjoyed that." Example: "Witnessing to all those girls on Daytona Beach over spring break really blessed my heart."

Bless the Food: Also "ask the Lord's blessing," "say grace," or "return thanks." The prayer given before a meal.

Edifying: Translation is "Constructive." Example: "Our visit to the rescue mission in the Bowery was very edifying."

Fellowship: Any time two or more born again people get together to talk, eat, and have fun. Example: "Come to the Young Adult College and Career Class Picnic for Food, Fun, and Fellowship." May also be used as a verb, as in, "Tommy and I fellowshipped so late last night that I missed my curfew and got grounded."

Go to the Lord: Translation is "Pray."

Harden: As in "Harden your heart. . . ." To stubbornly resist God (or your parents).

I Feel Led: Translation is "I want to. . . ." Example: "I feel led to take the youth group skiing in Aspen, Colorado, this year."

Lukewarm: As in "He is a lukewarm Christian." Indicates spiritual indifference or passivity. Not considered a compliment.

Share: Our major contribution to the 1980s. We were sharing long before it was made fashionable by West Coast self-actualized hot tubbers. Sharing allows us to spread news without being gossips.

Unspoken Request: For those times when you have a situation that requires prayer but is at the same time too personal for public disclosure. For example, say you put a dent in your father's car. That night at family altar, when your father asks if there are any prayer requests, you should say that you have an unspoken request. In doing so, you acknowledge that the situation requires prayer, but you avoid presenting the messy details to your father until after he's prayed for you.

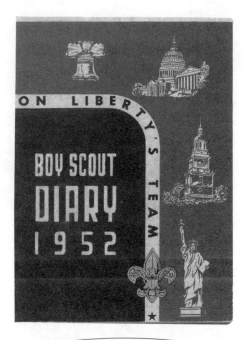

Give of Your Best: The Born Again Youth

It all boils down to choices. That's what life is all about for a born again person. You don't simply drift along. You *choose* your path. Every juncture in life, every issue you face, demands a choice. Do you choose God's way or the world's way? Will you choose Life or Death?

As you grow older, you are faced with a myriad of new choices. You already decided to be saved several years ago and now you're old enough to be mak-

ing a lot of new decisions on your own. Like whether to spend your offering money on forbidden entertainment—and then cover up the truth. Will you hang out in the gym with your friends during lunch hour, thus condoning the worldly rock and roll music played over the loudspeakers? Or will you be a good testimony and go outside to sit on the lawn reading your Bible? Will you roll up your skirt at the waist once you get to school so that it is short like everyone else's? Will you report wrongdoing, rule-breaking, and bad citizenship to the proper authorities?

It's also time for other decisions. You decide to get baptized. And then, one summer, you decide to dedicate your life to God.

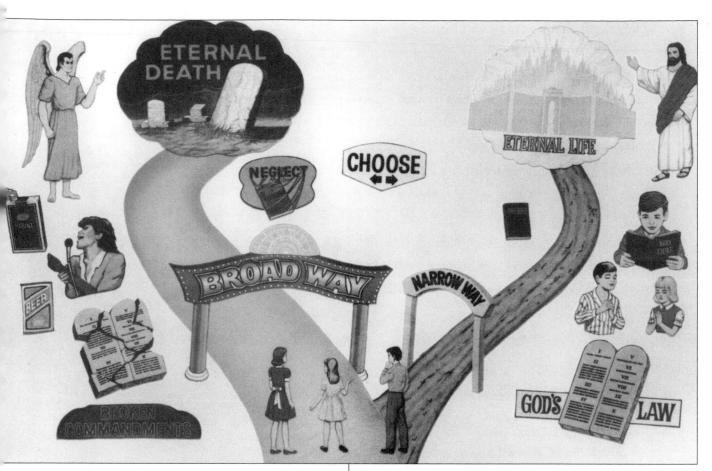

✳ Dedicating Your Life to God ✳

You remember the challenge as if it were yesterday. It may have been during Revival Week, perhaps after Missionary Conference. Maybe it was that time you heard the special speaker at Youth Group.

"Do you want to lead an ordinary, lukewarm, so-so kind of life, one with no lasting rewards? Or will you be sold out, fully committed to serving God, no matter what He asks you to do?"

Will you dedicate your life to God?

You think about it for months. Then finally, at summer camp (see "Bible Camp" in chapter 5), you decide. It's the last night of camp. Sad and happy at the same time. All week you've listened closely to the guest missionary and the evangelist. You've heard your counselor describe the joys of leading a committed life. You got up before dawn to hike to the top of the ridge for sunrise devotions. You've laughed and played and eaten with exciting new friends. Your heart is filled with gratitude and wonder.

It's time for closing campfire. Time to count your blessings and to consider all the things you've learned this week. Time to sit with that special friend for the last time.

Everyone places a fagot into the flames and gives a short testimony. The pastor steps up close to the fire and begins singing, quietly,

"Turn your eyes upon Jesus."

The entire camp joins him, singing in hushed tones and spine-tingling harmony:

"Look full in His wonderful face,
And the things of earth will grow strangely dim
In the light of His glory and grace."

You sit very still, very alert, straining to hear the next words. The pastor challenges everyone to reflect on God's love. What is the best gift that you could possibly give God in return for His love? Yourself. He wants nothing more, He expects nothing less. The pastor then challenges you. Do you have the courage to step forward for Jesus? Yes! You stand up (sort of surprising yourself) and walk purposefully toward the fire. You stand, head bowed, knees shaking, and like the mixed feeling of the hot on your face from the fire and the cold on your back from the night, you feel scared and confident at the same time.

You have dedicated your life to Christ. And now you are fully prepared to seek God's Will for Your Life.

Yield Not to Temptation:
Is This a Sin?

"For all have sinned and come short of the glory of God. . . ."

"There is none righteous, no, not one. . . ."

"The wages of sin is death. . . ."

"All we like sheep have gone astray; we have turned every one to his own way. . . ."

Sin is crucial to the born again person. Rather, the understanding of sin is crucial. Sin is not just *actions* (you do sinful things), sin is a state of being (you are a sinful person). You are born with original

sin. Then, as if that weren't bad enough, you start in immediately doing rotten things. There is never a mention of sin without the mention of salvation. Sin is the bad news, redemption is the Good News. The worse the sin, the greater the redemption. Interestingly, the people with the best testimonies seem to be the ones who managed to be the best sinners. Every Saturday night, you listen to the wonderful stories on *Unshackled*, a radio program about people who are lost in the depravity of bad music, alcohol, and fast living. Then they get saved and their lives are completely turned around. You find yourself wondering once or twice what it would be like if *you* could give a testimony like that. What if you had gone out to nightclubs and theaters, had fast friends, and stood around at parties holding glasses filled with tinkling

ice and booze? Your own testimony of resisting the temptation to steal some cookies—or repenting for the ones you did steal—would not make good *Unshackled* listening.

Even so, you are relieved God worked out a solution to the sin question. (See "Have You Accepted Jesus as Your Personal Savior?" earlier in this chapter.) And you pay close attention to the specific guidelines for righteous behavior outlined by your parents and church.

✳ "I Don't Go to Movies!" ✳

There are certain places you only have to look at to know they are worldly. A movie theater is one of those places—with its outside ticket booth to lure in the unwary; its broad, sloping floor leading up to mysterious doors beyond; its bawdy white lights on the marquee flashing to attract attention to some glittery Hollywood name like Rock Hudson or Marilyn Monroe or to a movie title like *Cleopatra*.

No, that's no place for a Christian to go—for a number of altogether incontrovertible reasons.

In the first place, you'd be giving your money to support the debauched Hollywood lifestyle and for those people to make more movies. They seem to be doing that anyhow, but not with any help from you, thank you.

In the second place, what if someone you knew were to see you paying your money at that little booth and walking in through those glass doors? If that acquaintance was someone from church, you might represent a stumbling block to him. If that acquaintance was someone from school, why, it might destroy your Christian testimony, which is vital to maintain at all times. (How many times, after all, have you heard the admonition to "abstain from all appearance of evil"? Being seen at movies is one of the main things this is referring to.)

In the third place, the movie itself is a sinful preoccupation. Not that you know this firsthand, of course, since you have never been to a movie. But those spiritual authorities on high (much higher than your parents) who know about such things, have

decreed movies off-limits, and you have no reason to question their judgment. Besides, we are admonished in Scripture to "touch not the unclean thing." What else does this mean if not movies?

The final reason—and the most compelling—for not going to movies is that your parents forbid it. That's a good enough reason for you.

Besides, there are other forms of entertainment right in your own home—Parcheesi, Old Maid, Candy Land, and, most notably, that new television set (not, alas, the first on the block) that has recently taken up residence in your living room, the purveyor of great programs like "My Three Sons" and "Leave It to Beaver." Now that, within limits, is a source of wholesome entertainment! (See "Hear No Evil, See No Evil" later in this chapter.)

✳ "I Won't Dance, Don't Ask Me!" ✳

As early as you can remember, you wanted to dance, to sway to the music. It was all right to sway as long as you had a stick in your hand and pretended you were conducting. You could skip or jump or gallop—as long as you didn't call it *dancing*.

You could get to high school without being bothered by this rule if it weren't for gym class. Every winter the teacher makes an announcement: "Don't change into your gym clothes because we're going to spend the next few weeks dancing."

You know what this means. You'll have to ask your mother to write you an excuse. You think about just not telling her (what mothers don't know can't hurt them), but it seems too risky. She'll find out from someone, somehow, and then grill you. And sitting on the stage watching the rest of the class have fun seems more desirable than the confrontation that would follow your cover-up attempts. If you're lucky, the teacher will let you run the record player.

Sitting out these gym classes wouldn't be nearly so bad if you understood what sin your friends were committing. You ask your mother why you don't believe in dancing. She seems to get a little nervous and, without looking up from her sewing, she says it's because girls and boys shouldn't be close or touch each other. She implies that something terrible will happen if girls and boys have a good time swinging their partners. This only confuses you more, and the next day you look at your friends more intently to try to figure out what it is they're doing that is leading them to destruction.

Finally you give up trying to figure it out. Maybe next year you'll be older and wiser. Maybe next year things will be more obvious.

✴ The Beat Goes On: Rock and Roll ✴

It hardly seems to matter what kind of music you like, your parents aren't going to like it. You have heard them attribute more of the world's problems to rock and roll music than any other thing, with the possible exception of "godless communism."

What's wrong with rock and roll music? Two things: the words and the music. Every young born-againer should know that the lyrics of rock music are inherently evil. Your father says they do nothing but glorify adultery, sexual perversity, rebellion against authority, and beer.

"But, Dad, I don't even listen to the lyrics."

Which is true, you don't listen to the lyrics. You don't need to—you have them all memorized! (All that memory training comes in handy.)

And if the lyrics don't get you, he says, the beat will! That rock beat makes young people do perverse things like stay out all night.

You have to admit that you've found yourself tapping your foot, even pounding the dashboard of your uncle's car when Buddy Holly's "Oh, Boy!" comes on the radio. Maybe those driving rhythms *could* make you want to stay out all night.

So what do you do if you're growing up born again and you happen to like rock and roll music? Or if some of your friends like rock and you feel left out because your parents won't let you listen to it? You have several options:

* Keep the volume very low.
* Buy an earphone for your transistor radio so you can catch the Top 10 countdown during Junior Choir practice on Saturday morning and the Golden Oldies in bed late Sunday night.
* Tell your parents that Ritchie Valens is a missionary from Argentina.
* Play your 45s at 33 1/3 to see if they sound any more spiritual that way.
* Pray that the Lord will let your parents develop a taste for Fats Domino and Elvis Presley.
* Start a Fanny Crosby fan club at school.

✸ Deal Me Out: Playing Cards ✸

They're compact; child-sized, in fact. They fit perfectly into the palm of your hand. They're shiny and pretty, with intriguing pictures and symbols all over the front and back. If you do it right, they make wonderful whooshing and clicking sounds when you shuffle them. You can play hundreds of games with them.

And they are strictly prohibited. Forbidden, verboten, off-limits.

Cards. Playing cards is sinful and people who play cards are sinful. But why this is so is not clear. Cards *seem* to be a reasonably sane adult pastime. The people you know who play cards are decent folks; they don't yell or hit people.

Besides (you ask), isn't it better to sit at home playing cards than to be out carousing around town in beer joints and nightclubs? Or, worse yet, a movie?

Your parents patiently explain why cards are wrong.

❶ Because the jack represents the devil. Or maybe the joker represents the devil. No, dear, it's the seven of spades that represents the devil. Never mind, you get the idea.

❷ Because cards are used in fortune-telling and other occult practices. You never know. What starts out to be a few hands of Go Fish could wind up as something really bizarre, like joining a lodge.

❸ Because card playing is a colossal waste of time. Time that could better be used reading your Bible or completing your Sunday School lesson for next week.

❹ Because playing cards can lead to a life of gambling. You may start out playing for matchsticks, but fifteen or sixteen years down the road, you could wind up a wasted, wretched bum, hanging out in Reno, desperately seeking that one fantastic hand that will put you back on your feet again.

So *no* cards!

But what about Old Maid?

And Authors?

And Flinch?

And how about Rook? Is Rook a sin?

> *Boys and girls, it is not nice,*
> *So never, ever play with dice!*

✳ No Dice: Gambling ✳

Listening to the advice of this poem could save you from spending the rest of your life hunched over those little cubes with the dots on them. Why are dice so bad? Consider the following:

❶ Shooting dice is a game of chance. Games of chance deny God's control over the universe.

❷ Shooting dice is gambling. Sure, those boys at school may be playing for baseball cards now, but soon they'll be moving into riskier territory, losing their lunch money this week and then their allowances for the next month. They'll probably also launch into other questionable activities, such as pitching pennies and shooting marbles for keepsies.

❸ Shooting dice is also called "shooting craps" and no Christian should use words like *crap*.

❹ A pair of ones is called "snake eyes"—and you can just imagine who that refers to!

5 The ancient Greeks and Romans shot dice, and look what happened to their civilizations.

6 Shooting dice is something you do in a back alley somewhere, which is no place for a Christian unless he is passing out tracts.

7 The soldiers at the cross cast lots for Jesus' robe, and lots were a sort of dice—so dice have a sordid history.

8 Finally, shooting dice is a deplorable waste of time, time better spent in spiritual pursuits. (See previous section on cards.)

There is some confusion, admittedly, as to why *shooting* dice is unacceptable, while *rolling* dice in games like Parcheesi and Monopoly is perfectly acceptable. In those latter games, of course, tossing the little cubes is only a means to an end, not an end in itself. After that, the distinction blurs a little—and you must be satisfied in the personal virtue of turning aside an ungodly pursuit, whatever the specific nature of its vice may be.

✳ Be Not Drunk with Wine ✳

"Dad? Did Jesus really turn water into wine?"

Dad looks happy you asked and proud at your obvious Sunday School familiarity with the first miracle of Jesus.

"Yes, He certainly did."

You press on. "But isn't it a sin to drink wine?"

Dad's face clouds and his brow furrows. "Well, yes, of course. But you see, the thing of it is, He didn't really turn it into *wine* wine. He turned it into, well, a sort of grape juice wine. As a matter of fact, it was more like grape juice. That's why it was okay."

Dad smiles at you, relaxed. You nod. The issue is only vaguely clear. You've never heard of grape juice wine, and no one you've ever heard of drinks

counted the tragic story of the fine young business-man who was enticed into taking one very small drink of whiskey. Immediately, he began a rapid downward spiral into depravity and drunkenness. He lost his family, his position, and everything he owned and wound up lying in a gutter, unwanted and despised.

You know you don't want to end up like that man, forsaken by your family and everyone who loves you. Still, the parents of some of your school friends drink, and they haven't ended up in the gutter. No one you know lives anywhere near a gutter.

You try one more time. "But why is it a sin to drink wine?"

Dad's tone this time sounds a little firmer. "Because our bodies are temples of the Holy Spirit. Drinking does damage to our bodies."

"How does it do that?"

"Whiskey kills our brain cells," he says emphatically. "Every single time a person takes a drink, he loses brain cells that can never be restored."

grape juice at weddings, like the one in Cana.

"Well, what about Jesus and His disciples at the Last Supper? Weren't they drinking wine then?"

"It wasn't really wine as we know it," he continues patiently. "They *called* it wine, but it wasn't really. It was—um—grape juice."

You nod again, not persuaded. You have often heard your parents inveigh against the demon of strong drink. Recently your pastor re-

WHO can measure
the SINISTER INFLUENCE
of just ONE "*social drink*"?

This is an interesting twist. Losing brain cells is something you *would* like to avoid.

"And besides that, the Bible says, 'Be not drunk with wine.'"

Dad is off and running now. His voice gets a little louder and he starts bouncing in his chair.

We don't drink or smoke or chew
And we don't go with those who do.
—*Traditional*

"If you don't want to get drunk, don't take a drink in the first place. Remember that. If you never have a drink, you'll never get drunk.

"And stay away from people who drink. Your cousin Grace used to say, 'Lips that touch liquor shall never touch mine!' That's a good thing for you to remember. You should avoid evil and every *appearance* of evil.

"That's why you never patronize grocery stores that sell beer or eat in restaurants that serve alcoholic beverages. Nor should you use cookbooks that include recipes with wine as an ingredient or instructions for how to mix drinks. What if a guest should think that you use these recipes? And even if you wanted to try a little sherry in your vegetable soup, you would have to go into a liquor store to get the sherry. And when you came out, across the street would be the preacher's wife on her way to her Bible class. And she would think that you're a closet drinker!"

Dad seems to be winding down. "That's what appearance of evil means. Avoid anything that *looks* wrong.

"Any more questions?" he smiles.

✳ That Evil Weed: Smoking ✳

Closely allied with the sin of drinking—so close that it is usually mentioned in the same breath, "drinkingandsmoking," almost as if it were part of the word—is the sin of smoking.

In fact, smoking is an example of one time when your church had the goods on everyone else. Your church knew smoking is a desecration of your body, the temple of the Holy Spirit, long before the Surgeon General's report was published. It doesn't take a genius to see that putting a weed between your lips, lighting it, taking a deep drag, and exhaling smoke

through your mouth and nostrils is not something Jesus would do, even if they had had Lucky Strikes in His day.

Still, there is something fascinating about the ritual. You wonder what a rolled, round cigarette would *feel* like. Apparently your baby brother wonders, too. A couple of times he has gone digging in a public ashtray only to have Mom snatch his hand out with the pointed exclamation, *"Don't touch that! That's filthy!"* It gives you a definite indication of where smoking stands in her book.

Nor do you have to wonder where smoking stands in your church's book. The adult Sunday School paper ran a fictional account—fascinating to your youthful eyes—of a church lady who was spotted as she drove down the street holding a slender white cylindrical object between two fingers. Word spread that she'd taken up smoking, and everyone was abuzz about her spiritually backslidden condition—until they learned it had been a white pencil, not a cigarette at all.

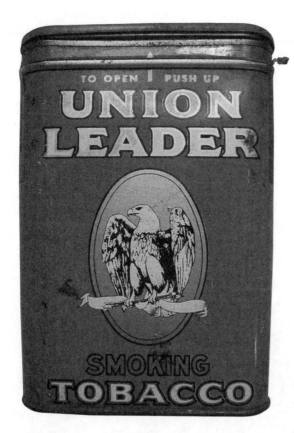

*Tobacco is a nasty weed
and from the devil doth proceed.
It picks our pockets and
burns our clothes
and makes a stovepipe
out of our nose.*
—Traditional

The lesson of the story, apparently, was not to gossip without foundation. The paper would certainly have backed the confirmation of wrongdoing, had it actually been a cigarette.

Not a person in your church indulges this sinful habit—unlike the church you pass on the way home, whose gentleman members lounge on the lawn taking a smoke. Sin could not be more blatant than this.

✳ Roller-Skating: ✳
A Semi-Approved Activity

Roller-skating is considered an acceptable form of entertainment if two conditions are met:

❶ The rink is rented by your youth group (or, more likely, the youth groups of several churches) for the evening, so that the party is "private," not open to the wrong element—unless of course you've invited them in hopes that they'll see you really *can* have fun. Then maybe they'll want to come to youth group meetings and Sunday School, where they'll get saved.

❷ Right before the last skate, everyone takes a break, sits down on the hardwood floor, sings a few choruses ("I Will Sing of the Mercies of the Lord Forever"; "Do Lord"; "Higher Hands"), and listens to a ten-minute devotional given by a youth pastor who hasn't skated all evening because he doesn't know how.

The evening starts in the church parking lot where you pile into a few waiting cars or the church bus (if it's not broken down). If you have a steady, you sit near the back of the bus to make sure no one can sneak up on you from behind.

Like baseball fans walking to the stands, your excitement builds until you've pulled the laces tight on your rented skates and pushed off with your left toe. Then you show off your stuff. Your power. Your speed. Your swivel and sway. Your charm. The bass beat and vibrato of the theater organ playing "Que Será, Será" brings out the best in you. (Why can't the church organist play this way on Sunday mornings!)

As at a dance (not that you've ever been to one), you can ask a girl—or be asked by a guy—for a song's worth of company. For five minutes your palm sweats into a stranger's. If you're feeling brave and if your partner isn't a stranger, you can even put your arm around someone's waist and have a guilt-free thrill. It's perfectly okay to do this as long as everyone's on wheels. As long as your feet may roll out from underneath you at any minute, you can't possibly get in any trouble, although you can, of course, get very black-and-blue.

If, by chance, the whole evening goes by and you've skated every skate alone, you leave the rink depressed, as if the home baseball team had lost the game.

Next month you go back. You never know when you might get lucky.

* Bowling: Is It a Sin? *

What in the world is wrong with bowling? Nothing, in itself. It's the bowling alleys that are suspect.

For one thing, nearly every bowling alley has some sort of lounge attached to it. And any sport connected to drinking, no matter how tenuous the connection, cannot be suitable entertainment for Christian youths.

Another problem with bowling alleys is that so many people there are smoking. After spending an hour or two in a bowling alley, you're going to come home smelling like cigarette smoke. And no Christian should smell like cigarette smoke. The Bible says clearly to avoid even the appearance of evil (see previous section "Be Not Drunk With Wine"), and you know instinctively this includes the *smell* of evil, too.

There is a third way bowling suffers from guilt by association. That is, many bowling alleys also include pool tables, and everyone knows pool is a shady game. Pool is for hustlers, for vulgar men in undershirts with tattoos on their arms, not for Christians. Pool has also long been associated with gambling, and you know where gambling will lead you. (If not, see previous sections on cards and dice.)

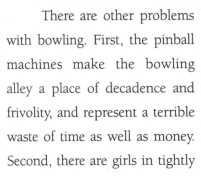

There are other problems with bowling. First, the pinball machines make the bowling alley a place of decadence and frivolity, and represent a terrible waste of time as well as money. Second, there are girls in tightly fitting skirts or pants, shamelessly showing off their endowments as they deliver the ball down the alley. It's just short of dancing—which is about as worldly as you can get.

Because of these unfortunate connections, bowling must defer to a game like croquet, which qualifies much better as an acceptably Christian sport.

✳ But Never on a Sunday ✳

Sunday is a day of rest. It's the Lord's day. This means that you spend all morning and all evening at the church. But what do you do all afternoon? That question isn't as easily answered as what *don't* you do all afternoon.

Your primary Sunday afternoon activity is sleeping. Eventually your body settles into a seven-day cycle. You never feel a need to nap on any of the other six days, but if you skip your Sunday nap, you're tired all the rest of the week.

Acceptable Sunday Afternoon Activities

- Take a nap
- Eat, do the dishes, eat more
- Read books from the church library:

    Sugar Creek Gang

    The Five Little Peppers

    Danny Orlis

    In His Steps

    Pilgrim's Progress

    missionary biographies
- Read Sunday School papers or *Moody Monthly* magazine
- Play church
- Play hymns on the instrument of your choice
- Write letters (preferably to missionaries)
- Play Christian games:

    Going to Jerusalem

    Bible Twenty Questions

    Bible Authors

    Bible Baseball

Forbidden Sunday Afternoon Activities

- Watch television
- Do homework
- Read school library books or *Reader's Digest*
- Talk to or play with non-Christian school friends
- Run and jump, especially outdoors
- Mow the lawn
- Ride bikes
- Practice your music lesson
- Play with dolls or trucks or any of your regular games
- Eat in a restaurant
- Drive farther than you have gasoline for

✳ Hear No Evil, See No Evil: Television ✳

Televisions can be dangerous because they bring the world right into your home. It's so easy—just a flick of the switch and you see what goes on in the living rooms of people who live much more interesting lives than you. That's the problem with TV. You know there's stuff on there that isn't fit for human consumption, but when you do watch it, you want more. You can't turn it off—but of course you do when your father walks in the room.

A few programs are always permitted, and *Leave It To Beaver* tops the list, except of course for the Billy Graham Crusades which you pray everyone in America watches. You love to see the altar call—all those people, just as they are, getting up out of their seats. And the miracle of television takes the message across the country. You thank God for television, and then you remember that Billy Graham isn't on every night.

Acceptable Programs	**Questionable Programs**
Leave It To Beaver	*I Love Lucy*
Father Knows Best	News by John Cameron Swazee
Wide World of Sports	(sponsored by Camel cigarettes)
Fury	*The Honeymooners*
Mickey Mouse Club (pending completion	Any program listed as a movie
of homework)	Any soap opera
I've Got a Secret	Walt Disney (no Sunday TV allowed)
Queen for a Day	*Your Hit Parade*
Roy Rogers and Dale Evans Show	*Milton Berle*
Sky King	Many more that you can't remember because you watched them only once

✳ *Turn Your Radio On* ✳

At your house, some of the best family times are spent listening to the radio. Although some of your friends aren't permitted to listen to the radio because the preacher who came to visit last winter said that Ephesians 2:2 proves that Satan controls the airwaves, your father says that God is stronger than Satan and Christian radio programs are okay.

Every afternoon when you get home from school, you have just enough time to fix some peanut butter and crackers before you sit down in front of the big radio in the living room to hear your favorite program. It always begins with the high-pitched voice of a youngster saying, "Aunt Theresa, please tell me a story."

The kind, mellifluous voice you love comes back, "What kind of a story?"

And the inevitable piping response: "Any kind!"

So starts another syndicated radio broadcast by Aunt Theresa Worman, whose voice you know and love, every day without fail. She weaves adventurous but homespun tales of—among others—Billy and Patty Bangle, who show just enough independent spirit to get them into mild scrapes and capture your sympathy, but not so much that they're not eager to attend to the grown-up wisdom of Mother and Father Bangle, which always prevails in the end. These loving parents mediate Bible truth to Patty and Billy in a warm and understanding way that even you can appreciate.

Even more, you appreciate your daily radio visitor. "Aunt Theresa," you want to say, "tell me another story."

But Aunt Theresa has finished her story, and now you'll have to wait until tomorrow.

Other Approved Radio Listening

All Back to the Bible broadcasts
Old-Fashioned Revival Hour
Night Watch
Sailor Sam
KYB Club
Ranger Bill
Tips for Teens
Aunt Bea
Unshackled

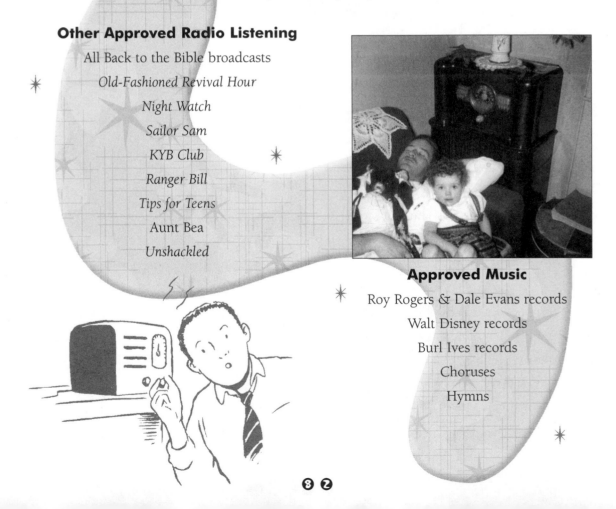

Approved Music

Roy Rogers & Dale Evans records
Walt Disney records
Burl Ives records
Choruses
Hymns

✳ Why Don't You Read a Book? ✳

At your house, the entertainment of all entertainments is reading. It's an even bigger recreation than eating! Mostly because eating is a social recreation and reading is personal recreation.

Your parents always encourage you to read because you're always good when you're reading and because (they say) books teach you good things about God. If they're the right books.

You love to read because books take you far beyond your yard and classroom to unspeakable adventures. Even the Bible (obviously your parents' first choice for your free-time reading) offers better tales of intrigue and passion than *Dragnet* or *Bonanza.*

But the best of the best is the Sugar Creek Gang series.

If there is an ideal Christian world, it must be within the pages of Paul Hutchens' *Adventures of the Sugar Creek Gang.*

You love the folksy style of the narrator, Bill Collins, who recounts the times his gang has run *kersmack!* into adventures in a way that suggests he's talking directly to you. "Say!" writes Bill. "I want to tell

folks call him "William Jasper Collins" when they're mad at him. Little red-haired Tom Till, who appeared in an early adventure and whose dad doesn't know the Lord, has become a seventh member of the gang.

Bill and the gang get involved in *bona fide* adventures; once they were even responsible for capturing kidnappers! Bill loves and obeys his folks and thinks his pastor and Sunday School teacher are swell. He hates it when anyone swears, 'cause the One whose name is used in such a terrible way is his best Friend. And he knows that the most important thing in the whole world is to be a soul-winner—which gives him the happiest feeling inside.

It gives you a happy feeling inside, too—at least while you're absorbed in the world of the Sugar Creek Gang.

you all about what was maybe the most exciting adventure that ever happened to us!" and you and he are off and running.

You have come to know and appreciate all the members of the Sugar Creek Gang: Big Jim, the biggest and the leader of the gang; Circus, the next-biggest, who can climb like a monkey; Poetry, the barrel-shaped member who recites poems by heart; Dragonfly, whose eyes are as large and round as his namesake's; Little Jim, a strong Christian and a swell little fellow; and Bill himself, a red-haired boy whose

Other Approved Reading

Bible
Sugar Creek Gang books
Danny Orlis books
Joy Spartan books
Felicia Cartwright books
Bible story books
Any book from Moody Press
Nancy Drew books
Hardy Boys books
The Five Little Peppers books
Grace Livingston Hill books
Trixie Belden books
Bobbsey Twins books
My Weekly Reader
Boy's Life
Highlights

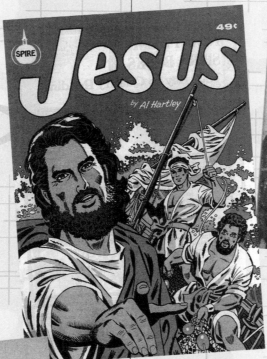

Unapproved Reading

Comic books
Kathryn Kuhlman books
Oral Roberts books
The Revised Standard Version
Dime novels, romance stories, crime stories
Gone with the Wind
Catcher in the Rye
God's Little Acre
Seventeen magazine
Fan magazines
True Confessions
Mad magazine
Confidential

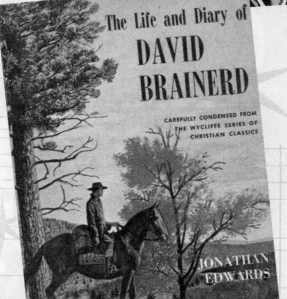

✴ Acceptable Exclamations ✴

Y ou must guard against the influence of your worldly friends. Without thinking about what they're doing, they take the Lord's name in vain. It's easy to walk down their path, which leads to destruction. But Satan works in even more subtle ways. If you aren't careful, you're likely to slip and start mincing your oaths. Both the law *and* the spirit of the Third Commandment are what's important. Don't think that you can change a letter or two and then use a word disrespectfully. God hears what you almost said, not what actually came out. Minced oaths to avoid:

Gee whiz

Gosh

Darn

Heck

Judas priest

The following words *are* acceptable. You may use them the next time your left hand, not knowing what your right is doing, gets hit with a hammer.

Fudge

Shucks

Piffl

Crud

For Pete's sake

E-o-w

Shoot

(contrary to what you might think,

this is not a minced oath)

Born Again Humor

Q Is this seat saved?

A No, but it's under conviction.

Q How do we know that God is a baseball fan?

A Because, right off the bat, the Book of Genesis tells us everything happened "in the big inning."

Q What two kinds of pedestrians are there?

A The quick and the dead.

Q Who was the man who had no father?

A Joshua, the son of Nun.

Q Where is smoking mentioned in the Bible?

A Genesis 24:64. "And Rebekah lifted her eyes, and when she saw Isaac, she lighted off the Camel."

Q Where does the Bible mention Santa Claus?

A Zechariah 2:6. "Ho, ho, come forth, and flee from the land of the north."

Q Who was the shortest man in the Bible?

A Shuhite ("shoe height").

Apocryphal Humor

Q Where are motorcycles mentioned in the Bible?

A "And David's triumph was heard throughout the land."

Q Where is tennis mentioned in the Bible?

A "And Joseph served in Pharaoh's court."

* Living for Jesus: The Born Again Young Adult *

* God's Will for Your Life *

The importance of finding God's Will for Your Life cannot be overstated. To an outsider, it may sound like a harmless oddity, a foible of born-againers, a mild fetish like eating white bread and Miracle Whip.

Think again!

Finding God's Will for Your Life is probably the highest priority of every born again person over the age of fifteen. It is a special way of grappling with all your fears and hopes for the future.

You ponder and agonize and pray that God will reveal to you this secret. You seek guidance from parents and pastors, you spend hours worrying with your friends, you read every book and article on the subject that you can lay your hands on. You envy to the depths of your soul any person who bears witness to having discovered God's Will and who is now pressing ahead to his own holy goal. You wonder, despairingly, if you are the only one to have been forsaken and if you will go through your entire life in a sort of Spiritual Limbo.

God's Will for Your Life can cover every aspect of

Fun
Dating
Personality
Parents
Manners
Looks
Education
Life's Work
Conversation
You and God
Wedding Bells
Military Service
God's Will

young only once
Secrets of
FUN & SUCCESS
Clyde M. Narramore, Ed.D.

living. What is God's Will about what I do Saturday night? What is God's Will about a car: Should I buy a new one? If so, what kind? What is God's Will about my summer job? Should I take the one that pays the most or the one that seems most spiritual?

God's Will for Your Life ultimately pertains to three major areas: marriage, college, and career. (Or, if you're a girl, marriage, college, and your future husband's career.) You must make the right choices. If you don't, it means that you won't really find God's Will for Your Life. So you must at all costs avoid college transfers, career changes, and divorces.

The biggest questions are:

Getting to know the will of God

by Alan Redpath

1 Does God's Will for Your Life mean full-time Christian service?

2 Does God's Will for Your Life mean remaining single? (A high-priority question for women.)

3 Does God's Will for Your Life mean serving God on the foreign fields?

Please note: It is very important to emphasize at this point that the issue is not so much whether the answers to these questions are yes. The issue is: Are you willing to obey God if the answers are yes? Every born again person realizes (hopes, prays) that if you are willing to sacrifice everything you want, then God will probably not require it.

If this all sounds like a Cosmic Catch-22, that's because it is. For example, you know you don't really want to be single, but you say that it will be okay if that's what God really wants.

God, as it turns out, is much smarter than we give Him credit for, and He is not really taken in by your "total sacrifice" routine. You don't figure that out, though, until you have wasted a whole bunch of time and energy. It's then you remember that when God stayed Abraham's hand from sacrificing his son Isaac, the issue was not the sacrifice, the issue was Abraham's obedience. Obedience is God's Will for Your Life.

* * *

Suitable Career Choices

Guy's

SUPERIOR

Pastor

Missionary

Missionary Doctor

Teacher

Evangelist

Bible Translator

Sacred Musician

Christian Bookstore Manager

Christian Radio Personality

Theologian

Amway Salesman

Holy Land Archaeologist

Shaklee Salesman

GOOD

Holy Land Tour Guide

Family Therapist

Consultant

Youth Pastor

Doctor

SATISFACTORY

Insurance Salesman

Accountant

Publisher

Realtor

POOR

ACLU Lawyer

Bartender

Blackjack Dealer

Game Show Host

Used Car Salesman

Bouncer

Movie Critic

Television Producer

Chiropractor

Politician

Hollywood Scriptwriter

Artist

Actor

"I was a night club entertainer . . ."

Gals

SUPERIOR

Pastor's Wife

Missionary Wife

Missionary Nurse

Teacher

Evangelist's Wife

Bible Translator

Sacred Musician

Christian Bookstore Manager

Mother

GOOD

Church Secretary

Secretary

Christian Writer

Librarian

Nurse

SATISFACTORY

Bookkeeper

Bank Teller

Computer Operator

Dental Hygienist

POOR

Aerobic Dance Instructor

Model

Game Show Hostess

Cruise Director

Elephant Trainer

Journalist

Studio Singer

Pastor

Evangelist

Theologian

Artist

Actress

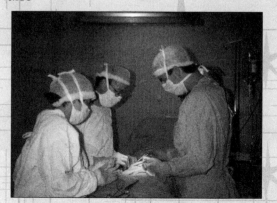

✳ Selecting the Right School ✳

Make a list of all the possible schools you may attend. Using the following criteria, assign the appropriate points to each school that you have listed. The school with the highest score is God's Will.

❶ If the school has "Bible" in the name, add 1 point.

❷ If it is an institute, add 1 point.

❸ If it is affiliated with your denomination, add 1 point; if it is affiliated with another denomination, subtract 1 point. If it is nondenominational, no points, unless your church is nondenominational, then add 1 point.

❹ If it is more than 100 miles from home (so you don't have to come home every weekend), add 1 point.

❺ If it is fewer than 300 miles from home (close enough to get home for holidays without a major hassle), add 1 point.

❻ If it has a major in your field of interest, add 2 points. If it has a major in your second field of interest, add 1 point.

❼ If it has a good male/female ratio, add 3 points.

❽ If it has daily chapel as a requirement, add 2 points.

9 If it has a Christian Work requirement, add 3 points.

10 If the president has ever spoken in your church, add 2 points.

11 If the school choir has ever performed in your church, add 3 points.

12 If your pastor, youth director, father, or mother graduated from the school, add 5 points.

13 If your fiancé or fiancée is attending the school, add 10 points.

14 If the school motto refers to Jesus, add 2 points. If it refers to God, add 1 point. If it speaks of truth and knowledge, subtract 1 point.

IMAGINE *Yourself* LIVING AND LEARNING IN THESE COMFORTABLE SURROUNDINGS

Student Parlor

Born Again Fashion for * Every Occasion!

FASHION HINTS

OCCASION	DRESS	FOOTWEAR	GLOVES	HINTS
Classes	casual dresses, jumpers, skirts, sweaters, blouses, (pantdresses, culottes are acceptable if regulation length)	loafers, sandals, flats		lengths of skirt vary with personal taste, but are not to be more than 2 inches above the knees in length.
Weekend Athletic Events	skirts, sweaters, sporty wool outfits	flats	leather or wool gloves	weather may determine snow shoes, and warm coat and bring a blanket
Church	suits, dresses	heels	yes	hat-optional
Weekend Programs, Receptions	dressy suits, dresses	heels	yes	
	formals – floor length not strapless	dressy heels	long or short	

AN OPEN
LETTER
TO BOYS
FROM A TEEN GIRL

* * *

✳ Dating and Sex ✳
(Or Rather, Dating and No Sex)

The subject of Christian dating raises more than just eyebrows among the adults of the church. It also raises fundamental questions: Is the expression "Christian dating" an oxymoron? What scriptural foundation, if any, exists for the practice? Did anyone in the Bible date? Eve didn't. Rebekah didn't. Samson did, but we all remember the trouble he got into.

You could argue that the verse "With an angry man thou shalt not go" implies the converse: It's all right to date ("go with") a man who keeps his temper in check. But this is stretching things too far.

Truthfully, whether dating is scriptural or not is a moot point. But everybody wants to date. So it's up to parents

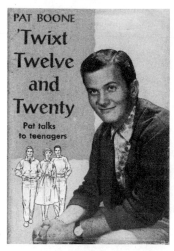

and the church to figure out how to make the best of it.

If you're a member of a large suburban congregation with a two- or three-bus fleet, you have a wonderful solution: the youth program.

Any youth program worth its salt (and it better be, or else what are the youth director and all his staff workers getting paid for?) effectively eliminates the need for dating, making it possible for two young people to meet, become friends, fall in love, get engaged, and be married without ever having been alone together or even in a car!

It also saves the young man hundreds of dollars in dinners out, basketball tickets, and concert programs. (The arrangement is strictly "dutch" until an official engagement announcement with photo is published in the local paper.) Popular girls are spared the trauma of picking just one guy to spend the evening with ("gang dating" is accepted and widely practiced). The not-so-popular girls are spared the embarrassment of date nights at home and nothing to talk about next week at school.

If you attend a small rural church, or any church whose entire youth population would fill a station wagon, you have big problems. Your parents and your church have developed dating guidelines designed to ensure that you will be safe from temptation at all times, mostly by guaranteeing that you never date.

Dating Guidelines

1. You may double date when you are sixteen.

2. You may single date when you are seventeen.

3. You may not car date until you are eighteen.

4. Your curfew is 11:00 P.M. on Friday and Saturday, 9:00 P.M. on school nights, and midnight on very special occasions.

5. You may date:
   —anyone who is a Christian, preferably someone who belongs to your own denomination.
   —anyone a relative or family friend fixes you up with (mostly because it embarrasses your parents to forbid these dates).

6. You may not date:
   —anyone who is not a Christian.
   —people with long hair, even if they say they are Christians.
   —people who ride motorcycles, even if they say they are Christians.
   —people with tattoos, even if they say they are Christians.

7 How to get a date.
Still a mystery.

8 How to refuse a date.
(Particularly important for born
again girls.)
Choose one:

"Thank you so much for asking
me. I'm afraid I can't go to the
movies with you. You see, I'm a
Christian."

"Thank you so much for asking
me. But I'm a Christian and we're
having our Youth Banquet on the night
of the prom."

"Thank you for asking me. But I'm a
Christian and we always go to church on
Sunday. Would you like to come with me?"

You will not need to refuse dates more than
twice. After that, word gets around and no
one asks anymore.

9 Where you can go on a date:
See previous section, "Is This a Sin?"

✳ The Youth Banquet: The Church's Answer to the Prom ✳

Y ou try to pretend that the prom doesn't even exist. You'd be uncomfortable there. You don't know how to dance, so you'd make a fool of yourself, tripping all over some guy, or moving left when you should be moving right, or just sitting on the sidelines dance after dance while your date went and found someone else.

You know you can't go, yet you imagine yourself being asked by some guy who'd understand perfectly why you are turning him down. He'd then

say that he'd rather spend the evening with you than go to a dumb dance, anyway; would you like to go out to a nice restaurant for dinner instead?

Of course, that conversation never takes place, so you're grateful that the church has a Youth Banquet every spring about the same time as the prom. They actually planned it that way so you won't feel bad.

You spend two days decorating the church basement with crepe paper and Kleenex flowers, and then you get dressed up in the new clothes you bought at Easter.

You want to have a date for the banquet, but it's not as essential as it is for the prom. In the youth group there are three girls to every guy and the guys can be divided into two groups: those who have steadies and those who

never invite anyone to anything. Those in the first group are not about to ask you, and if one in the second category did get brave, you'd probably have a rotten time.

You can always go to the banquet with the girls. At least then you feel safe. You know what to expect: A good time will be had by all.

✳ How Far Can I Go? ✳

Biff is the Special Guest Speaker at Youth Night. He's tall, tanned, and clean-shaven, with a square jaw, a blue blazer, and penny loafers. His wife, Cindy, is sitting in the first row, blond, petite, and pregnant. He *must* know what he's talking about.

The sanctuary is standing room only; the young are out in full force, praying for a new revelation: "We are no longer under the law, we are under grace." A few parents, poker-faced, are discreetly scattered throughout the audience. They are the guardians of truth, here to make certain that Biff presents only scriptural teaching.

They have no reason to worry about Biff.

After warming up the crowd with a few choruses and some jokes, Biff gets down to business. He lays his Bible, open, on the pulpit. Then he steps to the side of the pulpit and begins talking, earnestly, intently. He walks back and forth across the platform, always keeping his Bible within easy reach. He steps out to the edge, leaning precariously toward the information-starved, pathetically hopeful youth in the audience.

"How far can you go? How far is too far?"

His words hang in midair. Time stands still.

Kar-ack! Biff's hand suddenly smacks the pulpit.

"That's like asking, 'How long can I hold my hand in a flame without getting burned?' And that's *not* the question you should be asking! You *should* be asking the question 'How *far* from the flame should I stay?'"

The crowd senses what's coming next. A quiet rustle fans across the room as the disappointed young realize that Biff will not reveal a new dispensation and the relieved adults realize that Biff will not encourage any new leeway.

The text is "Flee youthful lusts." Great verse: clear, concise. It leaves no room for doubt or maneuvering. "Flee youthful lusts."

Biff retells the dramatic story of Joseph: how Potiphar's wife (the tramp) tried to seduce him and how Joseph steadfastly refused her attentions. Not once, not twice, but again and again. And finally, when she got really aggressive, he turned and ran away. He *fled!* (Leaving his coat behind was not so smart, though.)

That's what it means to "Flee youthful lusts." Just hope you aren't as unlucky as Joseph, who got arrested for doing so.

In case anyone is thinking about ignoring these warnings, Biff shares the story of Mike and Susie, two fine Christian young people who had planned to serve God as missionaries in New Guinea. But they didn't avoid temptation, so now Mike is working at a gas station and going to school at night while Susie takes care of their little baby. And then there's Bob and Marianne, two swell kids who thought they were in love. They ignored all the warnings and soon they went too far. Marianne discovered that Bob was just using her, but by then it was too late. She had already lost her most precious possession.

Throughout his talk, Biff has been

pouring out his heart. You can hear his voice break and catch just a glimmer of a tear as he tells of these poor kids who settled for second best. Now Biff gets quiet. He leans one elbow on the pulpit and looks intently into the audience. His eyes pass slowly over faces flushed with imagined danger.

"How far is too far? How far can you go?" (Pause.) "The next time you are tempted, stop and remember this: Jesus is always with you. He is with you in the backseat of that car. He is sitting on the davenport with you. He is walking in the woods with you. Stop and ask yourself: What would Jesus do?"

And with that final exhortation, Biff asks everyone to stand to sing "Have Thine Own Way, Lord." Parents and youths alike have learned beyond any shadow of doubt the answer to the question, "How far is too far?"

Remember now thy Creator in the days of thy youth.
Ecclesiastes 12:1

Commitment Guidelines for Born Again Couples

GO

CUTE ZONE
Sitting together in Sunday School
Sitting together on the church bus
Sitting together in youth group
Holding hands, in private

PDA ZONE
(Public Display of Affection)
Holding hands, in public
Sitting together in church
Sitting together in church
—thigh to thigh
—sharing a hymnal
—holding hands under
the hymnal

WARNING

COMMITMENT ZONE
Holding hands openly
His arm on back
of pew around her

MARRIAGE ZONE
Making out
Footsie under the table
Necking
Backrubs
Petting

STOP

ENGAGEMENT ZONE
Goodnight kiss
His arm around her shoulder, walking
Arms around each other, walking
Arms around each other, standing still
Arms around each other, sitting on a sofa

how to keep your HUSBAND HAPPY

how to keep your WIFE HAPPY

A CHRISTIAN GUIDANCE BOOK

Born Again Lingo

PDA (Public Display of Affection): A Christian school student handbook says it best:

"Students are expected to conduct themselves as Christian ladies and gentlemen at all times. Public displays of affection are in poor taste and are not permitted. Behavior unbecoming a Christian will result in counsel or discipline."

Unclaimed Blessing: Used to describe an unmarried Christian woman (young or old). Intended to be humorous.

THE KEY TO A
HAPPY MARRIAGE
ANNIVERSARY EDITION

Chapter Five

Faith of Our Fathers

This is the church;
This is the steeple.
Open the doors
And see all the people!
—Traditional

Faith of Our Fathers

No matter what our age or interests, the church had some program or other for us. Some things, like Sunday School and Morning Worship, were considered mandatory. Attendance at Sunday evening services and Wednesday night prayer meeting showed us to be more spiritually minded. (It also allowed us to see our friends.) Youth group, summer camp, and Vacation Bible School all catered to the special needs and interests of the young.

Parents were amazing when it came to these programs! Most of them volunteered for all sorts of duties that few folks in their right minds would do. Would you seriously consider volunteering to go to a mosquito-infested summer camp to cook for a bunch of kids? Would you spend hours developing lessons and handcrafts and cutting out flannelgraphs so you could teach twenty-five grade-schoolers in Vacation Bible School? Would you ever in a hundred years teach a mixed class of junior high kids?

But our folks did. They considered the church and all its programs to be a logical extension of the spiritual teachings begun at home. And they went out of their way to see that we not only got our spiritual teaching but that we also had every opportunity to have good Christian fun—well protected from the influences of the world!

Jesus Loves Me: Sunday School

✳ Opening Exercises ✳

When you arrive at Sunday School you hang up your coat and walk (don't run) down the center aisle of the sanctuary. There's no question about where you'll sit. Even if you're the first person to arrive, you know which pew your class is

He puts his big black Bible down on the front pew and picks up the birthday bank and the pastel pencils that have Bible verses printed on them. This is what you've been waiting

supposed to sit in for opening exercises. Every time you're promoted to a new grade, you get to move back one row.

Right at 10:05 the piano starts to play and the Sunday School superintendent makes you stand up and sing all the verses of a song from the hymnal. You know his favorites: "Onward Christian Soldiers," "Stand Up, Stand Up for Jesus," "He Lives," "Count Your Blessings," and you know what's going to happen right after the last chorus. He's going to ask one of the adults sitting in the back row to pray. Then the superintendent will read the Scripture lesson the Bible class is going to study.

for. "Are there any birthdays?" he asks. There always are and you always sing the religious and generic version of "Happy Birthday to You." Instead of addressing the song to a certain person—"dear Mandy"—you insert, "God bless you." That way one verse covers everybody who walks forward.

You're supposed to put pennies in the bank. One for each year of your age, but the grown-ups are allowed to cheat. They put in quarters or even dollar bills. You're sure that makes them a hundred years old, and isn't it nice that the Sunday School still gives someone that old a pencil? It makes you feel good.

After the superintendent reads the announcements out of the church bulletin and tells you about the upcoming Sunday School contest, he dismisses you to your classes and you walk (not run) downstairs into the church basement that always smells like an old suitcase.

✳ When the Roll Is Called ✳

The most important thing about Sunday School is being there. It's important for you, but more important for the Sunday School itself, which is always trying to outgrow its building. This preoccupation with attendance is evident in many ways:

✳ In every classroom you see an attendance chart taped to the wall. Down the left side is a list of names and each is followed by thirteen squares, one for each Sunday in the quarter. Every week you show up at Sunday School, you get to put a star or an animal or flower sticker after your name. At the end of the quarter you want to have thirteen stickers all in a row. You want to be the best Christian in the class.

✳ Some Sunday Schools have a more vigorous incentive program. They give out tickets that you are to take home and collect in a card box. The tickets, about an inch square, are printed on one side with Bible verses and pretty pictures—spring flowers or perching birds. You get a ticket just for coming, and when you have collected a lot of tickets, you can redeem them like Green Stamps. Here you have to make wise decisions. Are you going to keep trading in a few stamps for small items like Bible bookmarks, glow-in-the-dark crosses, the-Lord-is-my-Shepherd yoyos, and Jesus-is-the-Way combs, or are you going to save them up and get a brand-new King James Bible? You might say that the answer to this question separates the men from the boys. (Real Christians know all about delayed gratification.)

✴ A third incentive program is the Sunday School pin. If this method is employed, you only get your reward once a year, but then you are honored in front of everyone in opening exercises. The requirements for this medal are stiff. You must have perfect attendance, which has been defined with great grace. You're allowed to be absent on

account of sickness two Sundays a year. And you may go on vacation or visit your grandmother as long as you bring back proof that you attended Sunday School while you were out of town. This means you have to be brave enough to speak up and, in front of a class of strangers, ask the teacher for a visitor's card, which has to be authorized by the Sunday School superintendent. If, while out of town, you go to Sunday morning church only—not Sunday School—it counts for nothing. Even grace has its limits.

At the end of your first year of perfect attendance, you get the base of the Sunday School pin, which you can clip to your proud chest. You also get your first year bar, which gives you visions of

more, many more, dangling down so they jiggle when you walk. You try to imagine a pin with fifty bars—so heavy you'd get tired just wearing it. You laugh, but you know you're going to go for it.

✳ The grandest incentive program for Sunday School attendance is the annual contest. It's a game, really. The whole Sunday School—from cradle roll to Bible class—is assigned to be on one of two teams. Each team has a name and a captain and is given a twofold mandate: to be present every Sunday when the roll is called and to bring new people to Sunday School. On your mark. Get set. Go! Win! Win! Win!

Every year's contest has a different theme. It could be the Indy 500 or airplane races or baseball series. The teams might be represented by two model airplanes racing across wires strung from one side of the sanctuary to the other. Or by two model cars making laps around a track in a small-town version of the Indianapolis 500. Each week you eagerly check out your team's progress.

The losers have to feed the winners, which is to say that the losers have to organize, serve, and clean up after a Saturday night supper, held in the church basement. Oh, the losers do get to eat; they just have to do all the work, which really isn't a punishment because they're good Christians and

good Christians love being servants (even if they hate being losers).

But there are many variations on this standard Sunday School contest. One could be called Let's Break the Record. A certain Sunday is targeted as the day on which you're going to break the all-

Jesus Loves Boys and Girls

SATAN LOVES Empty SEATS

Then there were brought unto him little children that he should put his hand on them, and pray: and the disciples rebuked them.

But Jesus said, Suffer little children and forbid them not to come unto me; for such is the kingdom of heaven.

And he laid his hands on them, and departed thence.   — Matthew 19:13,14,15

Train up a child in the way he should go; and when he is old, he will not depart from it.
   — Proverbs 22:6

✳ Attendance is again emphasized at the end of each class, when you go back to the sanctuary for closing exercises. You sit in your respective pews and the superintendent points to the wooden attendance board that's nailed to the church wall. He tells you the good news: Today you have more people in Sunday School than you did last week. And you have more people in Sunday School than a year ago. Beating last year's figure is very important. It signals progress. It is proof of growth. It makes you feel like reaching for the stars. You go into the church service feeling proud and glad you came.

That's it! You now have the Sunday School enthusiasm down in your heart.

time attendance record. And the incentive is singularly fun: If you break the record, the person who brought the most visitors gets the honor of breaking a phonograph record over the pastor's head. (Please note: Some very old record albums are sheets of metal covered with black plastic. Reverend William Woughter of Big Flats, New York, can testify that such records will not break upon impact with a human skull.)

✳ Tell Me the Story of Jesus ✳

Once you're settled into your basement classroom, the teacher takes attendance and counts Bibles. She warns you to keep all four legs of your chair on the floor. And then it's time for the Bible story, which is what you've been waiting for. The flannel blue sky and green hills are on the easel board when you come into class. The story starts there, outside; Jesus and His disciples (made out of paper with flannel backing which makes them stick to the background) are walking toward the town, and Jesus stops to tell them a parable. The scene changes when the group arrives at the synagogue.

The teacher presses a second piece of the painted flannel sheet to the first. From the center of the board out toward all the corners, she smooths out all the wrinkles as if her palm were a hot iron. You wish you could do this yourself. You tried it once with two flannel pajama tops, but it didn't work very well.

You've seen the synagogue before. Last week the fat marble columns were King David's palace. Last month Shadrach, Meshach, and Abednego stood between them waiting for their sentence of fire. You're comfortable with the familiar. You wouldn't want the teacher to get a new synagogue, but you do hope that this story ends outdoors, with Jesus at the sea, so you can watch the teacher take the synagogue away and press the blue water on top of the green hills. It doesn't, though. The story ends abruptly when all the disciples fall off the synagogue onto the floor, and the teacher says that it's time to learn the memory verse. She repeats the words four times, then asks you to say it with her. All together now. Once. Twice. Three times. Now each person is on his own, and while everyone else says the verse, you flick the paint off the cement wall with your fingernails. Next, it's time to do the puzzles and answer the questions in the Sunday School quarterly. If you did them at home on Saturday night, you can be proud of yourself. If you didn't, you struggle along and wait for the buzzer to ring. Five more minutes and then you can go upstairs to the sanctuary.

We Gather Together: Church

* A Visitor's Guide to the Church Service *

When you walk into a born again church, first an usher shakes your hand, then he hands you a bulletin. The purpose of the bulletin is to give you an update of the various activities in the church and to outline the order of service. Every church bulletin uses a code (usually an asterisk) to indicate when the congregation should stand. This helps newcomers know basically what's expected of them, since standing up and sitting down are generally the only two movements made in the born again church.

For those of you interested in mastering the finer points of church behavior, we supply a more detailed code to help you determine when you may do what.

Every head bowed, every eye closed.

@ Appropriate time to visit bathroom or change pews.

@@ Appropriate time to casually look around to see who's there and who's not, who's wearing what, and who's sitting (or not sitting) with whom.

+ Appropriate time to rip checks out of checkbooks, unwrap gum or candy, tear paper to make a hat, or fold your Sunday School paper so you can continue reading the story.

** Time to meditate quietly, without fidgeting.

% Time to pay attention and listen intently.

Appropriate time to gather your Bible, papers, and family together and quietly sneak out the back door "to beat the rush."

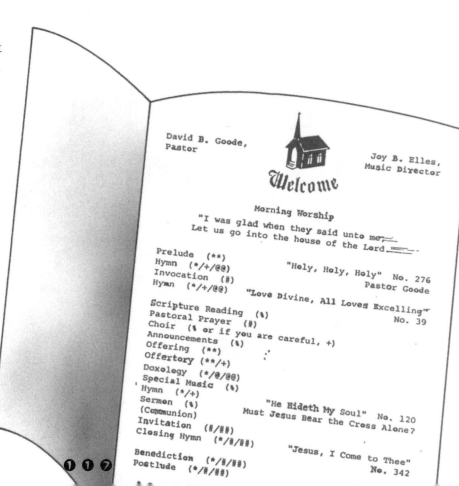

David B. Goode,
Pastor

Joy B. Elles,
Music Director

Welcome

Morning Worship
"I was glad when they said unto me,
Let us go into the house of the Lord."

Prelude (**)
Hymn (*/+/@@)   "Holy, Holy, Holy" No. 276
Invocation (#)   Pastor Goode
Hymn (*/+/@@)   "Love Divine, All Loves Excelling"
                                      No. 39
Scripture Reading (%)
Pastoral Prayer (#)
Choir (% or if you are careful, +)
Announcements (%)
Offering (**)
Offertory (**/+)
Doxology (*/@/@@)
Special Music (%)
Hymn (*/+)
Sermon (%)   "He Hideth My Soul" No. 120
(Communion)   Must Jesus Bear the Cross Alone?
Invitation (#/##)
Closing Hymn (*/#/##)
                            "Jesus, I Come to Thee"
Benediction (*/#/##)
Postlude (*/#/##)   No. 342

A Guide to Church Behavior

Preschool

DO . . .

- Keep the Life Savers candy Mommy gives you in your mouth.
- Sit quietly.
- Scribble on the back of the bulletin.
- Fall asleep in your daddy's arms.
- Listen to the sermon.

DON'T . . .

- Take Communion.
- Yell "OW! STOP THAT!" in injured tones to your mother.
- Punch your sister.
- Stand up in the pew and make faces at the people behind you.
- Play with your offering.

Grade School

DO . . .

- Quietly play Tic-Tac-Toe, Hangman, or Dots.
- Read your Sunday School paper.
- Find all the full-page colored illustrations in your Bible.
- Listen to the sermon and take thoughtful notes.

DON'T . . .

- Drop your hymnal.
- Stick your bubble gum under the offering plate as it goes by.
- See how big a bubble you can blow when no one is looking.
- Smuggle your gerbil to church in your pocket.

Junior High

DO . . .

- Fill out next week's lesson in the quarterly.
- Work on next week's memory verse.
- Look around for the cute boys (or girls).
- Listen to the sermon and take thoughtful notes.

DON'T . . .

- Giggle.
- Talk to your neighbor.
- Sing hymns in a lusty operatic voice, keeping a straight face when younger children turn to stare.
- Clean out your purse.
- Put on lipstick or Chapstick.
- Bring firecrackers to church.
- Eat Certs, butterscotch, or sticks of chewing gum.
- Bring Certs, butterscotch, or gum for your friends.

Choir

DO . . .

- Hold your music chest high.
- Keep your eyes on the director.
- Look like you're enjoying yourselves.
- Open your mouths while singing and e-nun-ci-ate your words.
- Put your offering in the plate. (The whole congregation can see you.)
- Listen to the sermon and take thoughtful notes.

DON'T . . .

- Rustle your music.
- Fall asleep.
- Put the final s on words ending a phrase until the choir director closes his thumb and forefinger. You'll sound like a punctured tire.
- Drop out on the high notes, forcing one or two sopranos to carry you through the climactic musical phrase triumphantly crescendoed by the whole soprano section in Tuesday night's practice.

High School

DO . . .

- Count the pipes in the organ.
- Daydream.
- Think about God's Will for Your Life.
- Study hairdos, necklines, and jewelry.
- Listen to the sermon and take thoughtful notes.

DON'T . . .

- Write notes on the offering envelopes and registration cards.
- Wave and smile at your friends.
- File your fingernails.
- Take off your shoes.
- Put your arm around your girlfriend.
- Plan your wardrobe for school next week.
- Look at photos in your wallet.
- Look at photos in your friends' wallets.

Adults

DO . . .

- Laugh at the pastor's jokes.
- Read the announcements in the bulletin.
- Read the Bible.
- Meditate.
- Pray.
- Listen to the sermon and take thoughtful notes.

DON'T . . .

- Plan next week's menus.
- Write a grocery list.
- Balance your checkbook.
- Catch up on correspondence.
- Review your appointment book for next week.
- Mentally rehearse asking your boss for a raise.

Games To Play in Church

The well-equipped pew contains all the equipment you'll need for several exciting games. For instance, the back of the bulletin usually has lots of space for writing. And if it doesn't, you'll find offering envelopes, attendance cards, and several stubby pencils (the kind you get when you play miniature golf).

One of the most popular church games is Hangman. Every evangelical Christian already knows how to play this game. Tic-Tac-Toe is another pastime that blossoms into national popularity on Sundays between 11:00 A.M. and noon.

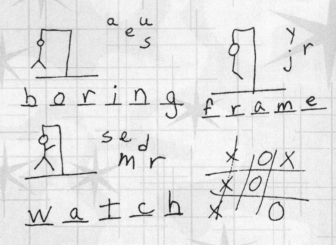

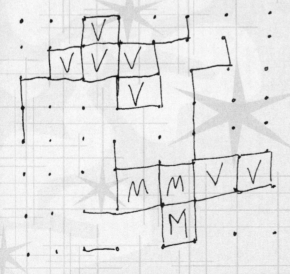

Another diversion especially designed for Sunday mornings is "Dots." In this game a piece of paper is covered with rows of dots. The object is to connect the dots and form boxes. You draw a line between two dots, then your neighbor does, and so on. (Of course, every time you pass the paper back and forth, you must take a long look at the preacher, as if you're actually listening to him.) You put your initials in every box you complete. At the end of the game, the winner is the person who was able to complete the most boxes.

While all of these games are exciting, they are for two players. What if you don't have a partner, or if Mom and Dad separated you because you were making too much noise? Well, in that case you can try these popular games for one:

Alphabet: This is a terrific game because it makes everyone think you're really paying attention to the sermon. And you are. First, listen for the preacher to use a word that begins with A, next with B, and so on until you've gone through the entire alphabet.

It's not always easy to get your Q, but if you're lucky the preacher will say he wants to ask a question, or he'll mention something about quality or quietness. The real problem letter is X, so you can cheat a little on that. Figure that any word with an x in it counts. After all, how often is your pastor going to say xylophone? You'll have a somewhat better chance with Z, since there are Zion, Zechariah, and Zacchaeus. The only problem is, by the time you get that far the sermon's almost over (or at least you hope it is).

Hymnal: All you need to play this game is a hymnal. Start thumbing through and read every title to yourself, adding "Under the Sheets." You'll come across such songs as "He Leadeth Me Under the Sheets," and "For Me He Careth Under the Sheets," or "I Come to the Garden Alone Under the Sheets." If you have a large hymnal, this game can definitely get you through a sermon or two. But be careful, because you might get the giggles, and laughing in church is one of the seven deadly sins.

* Why Women Can't Be Ushers *

If you're in the choir and sit on the platform, you have to wear a robe and/or sit behind a waist-high screen so that the congregation cannot see your legs. If your legs are bad, that would be bad. If they're good, it could be worse! Your church-hour activities are somewhat limited as you are being watched by the entire congregation, not just by the pastor.

If you're in the nursery, you can do whatever you please during the service, even jump rope. The elders have shown their concern for you by wiring the church so that you can hear the whole service.

They've also insulated the nursery so that they can't hear the babies who are crying because they are displeased with your care.

If you're in the pew, you might be thinking about most anything during the service, and you're grateful that only God can tell what's going through your mind. You try not to feel guilty and you don't, really, because you know that He knows that you wouldn't be here if you didn't love Him.

When you think about it, you see justification for the church's stand against women in positions of authority, but you've never been real clear on why women can't be ushers. So you ask the pastor and he tells you that there are several reasons for this policy. First, you wouldn't want strangers walking in to think that women run the church, which is what they might think if women greeted them and then took up the offering. Second, ushering is something

STEWARDSHIP

is the *calling*

of EVERY CHRISTIAN

"They . . . first gave their own selves to the Lord."
2 Corinthians 8:5

that men are good at, and this reason doesn't call for further explanation. Third, women ushers would simply be too distracting to the male parishioners sitting in the pews listening to the soft offertory music.

Trying to hide a blush, he goes on to explain that men are different from women in that they are tempted by what they see. He doesn't say the word lust but you know that's what he's talking about. He does use the phrase eye gate, and he says that this male weakness is the primary reason why women aren't allowed to take up the offering.

This makes no sense to you, but if he's right and if that's what these saintly men would think about if you were to take up the offering, you decide that it's

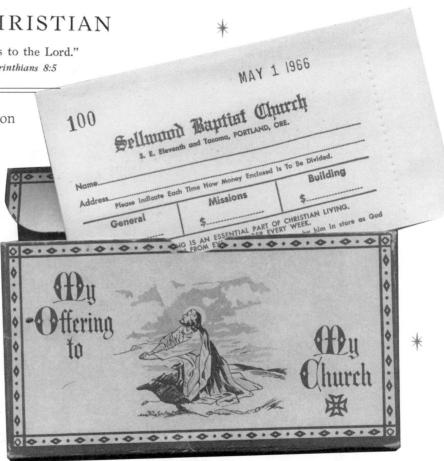

MAY 1 1966

100

Sellwood Baptist Church

S. E. Eleventh and Tacoma, PORTLAND, ORE.

Name............

Address............

Please indicate Each Time How Money Enclosed Is To Be Divided.

General	Missions	Building
	$............	$............

My Offering to My Church

all right with you just to sit in your pew. It even makes you think about volunteering for a year's stint in the nursery.

Christ for Me: Youth Group

You may hate going to youth group because its activities keep you from watching great television shows such as "The Many Loves of Dobie Gillis" or "Get Smart." Or you may love it because it's the only time you get to flirt with the girls who ignore you at school. Whichever it is, if you grow up born again, the church youth group plays a very important part in your life.

If you become active in the youth group when you enter junior high and stay active until your graduation from high school, at the end of that time you will have:

—Pulled 37 miles of taffy.

—Roller-skated enough to go between New York and Los Angeles four times.

—Made 14 trips to the nearest amusement park.

—Shot 98,712 holes of miniature golf.

—Consumed 112 pounds of toasted marshmallows and 23 gallons of hot chocolate.

—Spent the equivalent of two entire weeks singing "Kum Ba Yah."

—Been involved in at least six heart-to-heart talks (one per year) with the youth pastor.

—And, in between all the fun, you've had time for 600 hours of Bible study and another 125 hours of praying.

There are numerous other activities youth groups engage in, and even though some of these are regional in nature, the activities of most youth groups are interchangeable, as are the people who make up the group. People like:

Jack the Jock. Perhaps he's the captain of the high school football team, or maybe he's a benchwarmer on the basketball team. The important thing is, he's an athlete, and someone who tries hard to set a good example for the younger kids who idolize him.

Perky Patricia. This girl makes Mary Tyler Moore seem like a grouch. You've heard of 4-H? Well, Patty is 3-P—perky, pretty, and popular. In a group prayer she's always the first one to pray, and very often the last one, too. Her prayers undoubtedly bubble their way to God's throne. Several of her past boyfriends are now members of the youth group.

Holy Hannah. If born again churches had nuns, Hannah would be well on her way to being one. She gets upset if the group spends too much time running off to amusement parks and playing miniature golf. Every so often she gets up and makes a speech about how everyone ought to remember what the youth group is all about.

seniors

their characteristics and how to understand them

SCRIPTURE PRESS
SUNDAY SCHOOL LESSONS
BERNICE T. CORY, EDITOR-IN-CHIEF

Nick the Nerd. (Formerly known as Craig the Creep and Jerry the Jerk.) Poor Nick! When the youth group is going skating he shows up at the miniature golf course. When the lock-in is Friday night, he shows up on Saturday. When (and if) you try to talk to your "cool" friends about Jesus, they're sure to say something like, "Oh, yeah. This Christianity stuff is for losers." And when they say it they'll be thinking of Nick.

Gary Goof-Off. He pretends he hates the youth group, but that's just because he wants to be cool. He never opens his Bible, delights in throwing spitwads and shooting rubber bands, and is personally responsible for many bruises and abrasions every time the group travels to the roller rink. Gary is good for mainly one thing—to use as a bad example.

Frustrated Francine. Francine may love the Lord, but her primary goal insofar as the youth group is concerned is finding a boyfriend. It's not that she's unattractive, she's just overanxious and a bit heavy-handed. Even the boys who would like to ask her out won't do it, because they know the other boys would tease them about going out with her. Francine's frustration is undoubtedly compounded by the fact that in every youth group, girls outnumber boys by a large margin. Why? Nobody really knows.

Hash Chorus*

Every day with Jesus
I'll be walking down the King's highway;
Tell me the old, old story
I love it better every day, hallelujah!
I will make you fishers of men
If you'll only follow Me.
Hallelujah, what a Savior
I'm from sin set
You're from sin set
We're all from sin set free.

—Traditional
*created by bits and piesces of many songs

Prayer Meeting

Sweet Hour of Prayer:
Prayer Meeting

Midweek prayer meeting is for the truly faithful who take the Word seriously; we forsake not the assembling of ourselves together. Unlike other services, you can predict who will be at prayer meeting. Church members fit into one of two categories: those who wouldn't think of missing the service and those who always intend to come but seldom do.

There won't be any surprises in the music, either. You always sing the old songs you've known by heart since before you could read. If you're not yet a great piano player, here's your chance to get some public practice. You know you can handle songs you're familiar with.

This is one service when the pastor's talk is brief, just a short course to get you through the rest of the week. Then comes the real stuff—the testimonies and prayer requests. (And you thought support groups were invented in California.) "What has God done for you this week?" the pastor asks.

You wait through a long pause, and then two people stand up and talk at the same time. The shyer person, Mrs. Harris, sits back down. Mr. Richards keeps talking, not even aware of her presence. Last night he was driving home from work and the car right in front of him was broadsided by a drunk driver who didn't stop at the red light. Just think, it might have been him, but praise the Lord it wasn't. God protected him. He gives all the details and then sits down.

A voice behind you says, "Amen," as if it were the end of a prayer. After a pause, Mrs. Harris stands up again. You're embarrassed for her because her skirt is caught up between her legs. She speaks in vague generalities. "Sometimes you're on the mountaintops but sometimes you walk through the valleys. You wonder why you have to get down so low and then you're brought back to the Scripture, 'I will fear no evil for God is with me, his rod and his staff they comfort me.'" You know she cries easily and you know she's going to now. She ends quickly: "I thank Him for His Word, and I just want to say once again that I stand on His promises. They never fail. I want to go all the way through with Jesus. Praise His name."

The same man behind you says, "Amen." And you wait for what seems like forever for someone else to say something. It's the pastor who says, "Anyone else?" He waits awhile longer and two more people testify. Finally he says, "Now for prayer requests."

Now the group gets talkative. Maybe it's because everyone knows what he wants from God; maybe it's because you don't have to stand up to give a prayer request. You can just speak out—one at a time, of course. Everything here is done decently and in order.

There are the sick among us—those who never get better and those who always do. There is thanks for healing. There are the requests for traveling mercies, for guidance, for success, for souls. There are the unspoken requests.

When it's time to pray, you kneel—facing the back of the church. Who needs—or wants—soft kneelers when you can turn around, put your knees right on the cold tile floor and rest your arms on the pew seat, all toasty warm from your own body heat? If you're an old saint, you really do kneel, back slightly bent, elbows on seat, and head in hands. In this position you never fall asleep.

If you're not quite old or saintly, you sit right on the floor and bury your head in a little nest you make with your arms. Your nose is right against the seat. You can't tell whether you love or hate the smell, as you're not sure what the scent is. It could be the wood itself. It could be the furniture wax they put on it. Or it could be the smell of people, the hundreds, maybe thousands who've warmed this bench. For a minute you think about this and weigh the possibilities. Is this why they're called pews? Then you remember you're supposed to be praying. You listen to the person beseeching the Lord out loud and amen every request, but that doesn't last long.

You've made yourself comfortable, so comfortable, so very comfortable that you don't hear another word until the pastor says his final and loud Amen.

Vain Repetitions

"But when ye pray, use not vain repetitions, as the heathen do; for they think that they shall be heard for their much speaking." –Matthew 6:7

Vain repetitions. Surely these are not to be found within the province of those who have grown up born again! Or are they?

Not that you'd indulge in prayer wheels, strings of beads, written prayers, or other "prayerphernalia." But have you ever found yourself rattling off pious phrases while your mind replays the exciting finish of last night's basketball game? Or have you ever nudged your companion in a restaurant to ask, "Er, did you happen to notice—have I said grace yet?" Aha! Caught yourself in the act.

Of course, it's not the words that make a repetition vain. The words may be quite meaningful. It's not even the repetitions. It's the mindlessness of the renderings. Consider these examples:

OurmostgraciousHeavenlyFatherthankYouforthisdayandeverythingYou'vedoneforus.

Bewithallthemissionariesintheforeignfields.

BlessthisfoodthatitmaynourishourbodiesandstrengthenusforThyserviceLord.

BewithallthesickDearGodandifitbeYourwillraiseSisterSo-and-Sofromherbedofaffliction.

Bewithusthroughouttherestoftheday.

GodblessMommyandDaddyandGrandmaandGrandpaandSusieandBillyandBoxerandMittensand GoldiethegoldfishAmen.

VBS is Fun!

✳ Daily Vacation Bible School ✳

The best things about Bible school are refreshment time, being with your friends, and the fact that it's over by noon on those warm summer days.

The worst thing about Bible school is doing handcrafts, which show you up every year as thick-fingered and unskilled. You could get away with the "baby" crafts, such as the dyed-macaroni necklaces, baskets made from Popsicle sticks, and painted-tin-can pencil holders.

But last summer you proved yourself a cretin with your clay model of David, the shepherd boy. And how could you have hoped to compete with your friends' stained-glass-window pictures?

Only the Scripture plaque from two years ago, made of plaster of paris that just needed paint, didn't turn your face hot with humiliation. It was a down-right inspiration to paint the words of Jesus in red—"I am the way, the truth, and the life"—when everyone else painted them black.

That plaque in all its evangelical glory—because, despite your shortcomings, you *can* paint within the lines—will adorn your dresser for years to come, a sample of one successful Bible school project.

Sunshine Mountain
Do You Know All the Motions?
❶ *Climb, climb up sunshine mountain,*
❷ *Heav'nly breezes blow;*
❶ *Climb, climb up sunshine mountain,*
❸ *Fac-es all a-glow.*
❹ *Turn, turn from sin and doubting,*
❺ *Look to God on high;*
❶ *Climb, climb up sunshine mountain,*
❻ *You and* ❼ *I.*

✳ Fishers of Men ✳

✳ Missionary Conference ✳

One of the missionaries' greatest fears is that you will forget them. You mustn't do this because they need your money, your letters, your leftovers, your used postage stamps, and your prayers. To guarantee that they'll be remembered, missionaries travel from church to church putting on slide shows. This travel schedule is called *deputation*. You wonder why and decide that missionaries must be God's deputies. From what you can figure, giving this slide show is the missionaries' idea of a vacation, as it's what they come back home to the States to do.

Missionaries who come to your church want to take you on a trip to the foreign land they've come to love. They can't put you in their suitcases, so they show you pictures and bring you curios. They recite John 3:16 in the language they've learned, and the missionary's wife wears a funny-looking dress. After you've sung several missions songs that remind you of the need in the regions beyond, the missionary narrates the slide show and you try to stay awake.

You see the Atlantic Ocean from the window of an airplane. You know the missionaries are sad to say good-bye to their homeland, but that emotion pales in light of the excitement they feel about the challenge that is ahead of them. The wing of the plane cuts the view of a corner of the ocean. Next slide please.

You see the long coastline of their adopted tropical country. You just know they're going to feel at home there. Next slide please.

You see a map of their field, which is not a field but a country. They walk close to the

screen and point out the capital and four mission stations. The needs are so great and the laborers are so few. Next slide please.

You see a crowded street of the capital city which is teeming with young people who've moved here because they were restless with the slow life in the villages. Some of them find work and make enough money to support themselves and send money back to their families, but some are engulfed in the darkness. . . . Next slide please.

You see the missionary's wife smiling into the camera. She's standing alongside a Land Rover that is stuck in a mudhole that is really a road. You don't worry. You know everyone is going to make it to the village. Next slide please.

You see the missionary compound—a lot of white stucco buildings surrounded by grass that's "mowed" by boys wielding sickles. Next slide please.

You see flora and fauna that you wish grew or grazed in your own backyard. Next slide please.

You see hospital patients who seem delighted to have pictures taken of their tumors and elephantiasis sores. You close your eyes and wait for the missionary to say, "Next slide please."

You see the beaming, gleaming faces of the nationals as they pose, lined up in front of their church. You look at all the women to see if any are wearing one of your mother's old dresses. Next slide please.

You see the Bible school students on graduation day. These men are our hope for tomorrow. They're going to take the Word to their own people who are not black but white with harvest. Next slide please.

You see the sun set behind the horizon. Day is done. Gone the sun. This slide belongs in *National Geographic* and makes you wonder if you have a call to the mission field.

Lights please.

For You I Am Praying

Missionaries on the foreign fields need more prayers than people who live here in America. To make sure they get these prayers, they are paired with prayer partners.

If you have a prayer partner you must:

* Display the missionary's prayer card or photograph where you will see it every day. You can put it on the refrigerator door, lean it on the windowsill above the kitchen sink, or slide it between the mirror and its frame in your bedroom.

* Breathe a prayer for your missionary every time you see the prayer card. You are also to pray for him or her every night before you go to sleep and every Wednesday night at prayer meeting.

* Write your missionary a letter of encouragement shortly after you get your assignment and then within ten days of receipt of any reply, which will most likely be a form letter. Missionaries usually don't have time for personal responses.

* Send a birthday card to your missionary. To remind you, birth dates are printed on prayer cards.

✳ Packing Missionary Barrels ✳

If you are a missionary you are privileged to labor unrewarded. If you are not a missionary you are privileged to send your castoffs overseas. What do the missionaries need?

Clothes. The women of the Missionary Society take very seriously their responsibility for packing the missionary barrels or boxes. The decisions are crucial, but the women never agree. A summer shirt is worn through on the collar and thin as gauze across the shoulders. Mrs. Smith thinks there's still a lot of wear left in it. Mrs. Kamp thinks it isn't worth the postage on a slow boat. Mrs. Smith always wins because everybody agrees that some clothes are better than no clothes, even at the Equator. But this rule does not apply to shorts or low-cut dresses, even if they have never been worn and still have the store tags on them.

Bandages. At work meetings the women in the Missionary Society take out their frustration on sheets that have been toe-poked and washer-agitated to death. Some people might throw these sheets into the ragbag, but Christians don't. They collect them and then gather together to rip them into two-inch strips which they roll like the Ace bandage that's stored away in the medicine cabinet.

The sheets have lost their identity. They are no longer sheets but hospital bandages. At these work meetings the women used to work—yank and tear—but now they've learned that you can do your part and have fun at the same time. It works like this: With scissors one person cuts a notch every two inches across the top of a sheet. She finds a partner and each grabs ahold of every other notch (one for you and one for me, one for you and one for me). Then they have a tug-of-war, ripping a sheet into strips in one fell swoop.

Hospital gowns. Men's white shirts are also lifted to greater heights in the hands of the Missionary Society. The shirts are stripped of their collars, cuffs, and buttons and made into hospital gowns with ties added at the neck. As they say, the front shall be the back and the back shall be the front (or something like that).

Used printed material. In the hands of missionaries, the pretty pictures on the front of greeting cards become prizes for children. Leftover Sunday School papers tell African children not to steal cookies from a jar.

Used tea bags. Rumors abound that missionaries, who are temperate in all things, are especially fond of weak tea.

A missionary conference might last three or four days and feature as many different missionary speakers. They wait until the last service to ask you for the ultimate sacrifice. Is God asking you to lay down your life for His service?

So Send I You

So send I you to labor unrewarded,
To serve unpaid, unloved, unsought, unknown,
to bear rebuke, to suffer scorn and scoffing.
So send I you to toil for Me alone.

So send I you to band the bruised and broken,
O'er wand'ring souls to work, to weep, to wake,
to bear the burdens of a world a-weary.
So send I you to suffer for My sake.

So send I you to loneliness and longing
With heart a-hung'ring for the loved and known,
Forsaking home and kindred, friend and dear one.
So send I you to know My love alone.

So send I you to leave your life's ambition,
To die to dear desire, self-will resign,
To labor long and love where men revile you.
So send I you to lose your life in Mine.

So sent I you to hearts made hard by hatred,
To eyes made blind because they
            will not see,
To spend, tho' it be blood—to spend
            and spare not—
So send I you to taste of Calvary.

—E. Margaret Clarkson

Revive Us Again: Revival Meeting

to as "spiritual hitmen." This had to be explained to you, and you were told that they do what the minister wants to do every Sunday but doesn't dare.

If you're lucky, the evangelist can sing and his sweet wife is very talented. With the greatest of ease she can slip from the piano to the organ to the marimba to the accordion to crystal goblets. You wish she could play the saw but she can't. You want to buy one of their records. On the front of it there is a picture of the two of them standing on the edge of a forest. These albums are on sale every night (but never on Sundays) in the vestibule. Yes, you're sure you want to enjoy their music all year long. If this couple ever settled down and stayed in one town long enough to get real jobs, the wife could get work at a roller-skating rink. She could play the organ there,

Twice a year, in the spring and in the fall, your church needs to be revived. The Spirit wants to break through and He seems to do this best when an evangelist from out of town comes and preaches at you every night for a week. You've heard these traveling evangelists being referred

although you have no idea what he would do for a living.

Revival meetings (now more fashionably called "Special Services") are held for two purposes: to get sinners saved from the fire of hell and to get Christians fired up. On any given night you might walk into the church feeling sure that you're a Christian. But by the time the sermon is over you're not so sure. After four verses of "Oh, Why Not Tonight?" you're quite certain that you've been living a lie. You know you should go forward, but you don't want to. It's pride, you realize. You shouldn't let pride stand between you and the Lord.

"Now I lay me down to sleep.
I pray the Lord my soul to keep.
If I should die before I wake,
I pray the Lord my soul to take."
—Traditional

Ye Watchers and Ye Holy Ones: * Watch Night Service *

B y asking people what they are doing on New Year's Eve, you can tell whether or not they're real Christians. If they stay home and watch the ball fall on Times Square or if they go to parties, make no mistake—they are not in the fold. Real Christians go to church for the Watch Night Service. This is the only service that has an intermission—for fellowship, which is to say food.

The festivities start at 9:00 P.M. To keep the children from going to sleep right away, you sing for forty-five minutes. Everyone present has a chance to choose a favorite. You sit for a few songs, then stand for one, then sit for a few more, then stand for another. You do this because adults won't stop and sing "Bend and Stretch," especially at a church service. Between songs, people give testimonies or reports of God's mercies over the last 365 days.

After you've sung yourself hoarse, you watch a movie—a Christian movie produced by a Christian company that employs Bible-believing actors and actresses. The family portrayed reminds you of Beaver Cleaver's, except this family talks about God a lot.

They win their neighbors to the Lord, and the movie ends with both families walking into church together. The lights come on and everyone goes downstairs to eat leftover Christmas cookies until 11:15 when you go back upstairs for a devotional long enough and sober enough to be a real sermon.

You don't fall asleep because you want to see the new year in. Every five minutes you turn around and look at the big round clock on the back wall. You can't wait for the hands to reach twelve, and when they do you're disappointed that everything feels the same. No bells ring. No lightning flashes. Jesus doesn't return. You just gather in a circle, hold hands, and sing "Blest Be the Tie That Binds" instead of "Auld Lang Syne."

You make yourself a promise. Next year you're going to sneak out and ring the Sunday School buzzer right at the stroke of midnight.

Sing Them Over Again to Me...

Most born again children spend hours singing and listening to choruses,
from nursery all the way through high school. How many do you remember?

"The birds upon the tree tops"

"Wide, wide as the ocean"

"Jesus loves the little children"

"One door, and only one"

"On Sunday I am happy"

"Praise Him, praise Him, all ye little children"

"There were twelve disciples"

"'Tis G-L-O-R-Y to know that I'm S-A-V-E-D"

"Are we downhearted?"

"Jesus loves me, this I know"

"Oh! Say but I'm glad"

"Thy Word have I hid in my heart"

"We're going to the mansion on the 'Happy Day' Express"

"Mine, mine, mine, mine, Jesus is mine"

"This little light of mine"

"Zacchaeus was a wee little man"

"Behold! Behold! I stand at the door and knock, knock, knock"

"Oh, be careful little eyes what you see"

"Whisper a prayer in the morning"

"Heavenly sunshine, heavenly sunshine"

"I may never march in the infantry"

"Deep and wide, deep and wide"

"Running over"

"Dare to be a Daniel"

"Rolled away, rolled away, rolled away"

"The wise man built his house upon the rock"

"Only a boy named David"

"Isn't He wonderful?"

"Everybody ought to know"

"Give me oil in my lamp"

I'd Rather Have Jesus: ✳ Bible Camp ✳

Why let your kids sit around all summer getting bored when they could be out in the fresh air, learning new skills and making new friends? And best of all, they can get to know the Lord in wonderful new ways!

Why let your kids sit around all summer getting bored, when they could be out in the fresh air, learning new skills and making new friends? And best of all, they can get to know the Lord in wonderful new ways!

CAMP IDRAHAJE

A summer camp for boys and girls between the ages of seven and seventeen. A wonderful variety of activities designed to give your child an unforgettable week of fun, recreation, and solid Bible teaching.

SCHEDULE
Monday morning: Check in. Get your cabin assignment and meet your counselor and cabin mates.
First meal (Monday lunch): Cold cuts, potato salad Jell-O for dessert

1:45-4:30 Recreation (Canteen open) Activities are scheduled according to age group and gender. See your counselor for details. Crafts-Swimming-Boating-Baseball-Volleyball-Archery

DAILY SCHEDULE:
6:00 a.m. Reveille
           Cabin Devotions
7:00   Breakfast
7:30   Clean cabin
           (for inspection)
8:00   Personal Devotions
8:30   Bible Class
           (in the Tabernacle)
9:00   Morning Break
           (Canteen open)
10:00   Bible Class
10:30   (divided by age group)
12:00   Lunch
1:00 p.m. Rest time

5:00   Supper
6:00   Free time
           (Canteen open)
7:00   Chapel (in the Tabernacle. Attendance required; girls must wear dresses.)
8:30   Free time (Canteen open)
9:30   Evening Devotions
10:00   Lights Out

Saturday morning: Check out. Say good-bye to all your new friends, get everyone's ...in your autograph book, get everyone's

✳ What to Pack for Camp ✳

All campers: Bible, notebook, pen or pencil, flashlight, towels, washcloths, soap, toothbrush, toothpaste, bedroll or sleeping bag, and rubber sandals.

Boys: Sports clothes (blue jeans, sneakers, T-shirts), dress clothes (one pair dress pants, one dress shirt, one tie, dress shoes), bathing trunks, pajamas, and robe.

Girls: Sports clothes (no sleeveless blouses; no pants above the knee; slacks or pedal pushers only; no halters; no suggestive clothing), dress clothes (dresses must be worn to all Chapel services), bathing suits (no two-piece suits permitted), sleepwear, and robe.

✳ Special Events ✳

In addition to the flurry of intercabin sports competitions, Bible memory contests, crafts, chiggers, and sunburn, Bible campers have a few special activities uniquely their own.

Stunt Night (or *Talent Night*). Held on Thursday during six o'clock Free Time. During the week each cabin develops a skit or special talent to present to the entire camp. The best skit or talent (as voted by a special panel of judges) wins a one-dollar gift certificate to the canteen for each person in the cabin.

Late-Night Hike. For high school campers only. After Chapel, campers gather on the recreation field for a midnight walk through the woods surrounding the camp. (Editor's Note: This event is a mysterious acknowledgment of the budding sexuality of the campers. Remember, these same boys and girls who are being flocked together for a moonlight walk through shadowy woods weren't permitted to swim with each other earlier in the day.)

Pioneer Girls
CAMP CHERITH

Date Night. At Bible camp, campers are always organized by cabin, making the task of keeping the sexes separate much easier. Thus, mealtimes are always spent with the kids from your cabin. That's why Date Night is so special. On Date Night (usually Friday night), you get to sit anywhere you like and with whomever you choose. Boys are encouraged to choose a Special Someone to escort to Date Night. And girls spend the entire week scouting for a Special Someone of their own. Obviously this event can ruin a perfectly good week at camp.

Campfire Night (sometimes called *Fagot Service*). After Chapel, all campers change their clothes and meet on the assembly field for a short hike up to the campfire for the final service of the week (see previous section, "Dedicating Your Life to God"). After a few songs, each camper is encouraged to come up to the fire and throw in his fagot as he gives his testimony (what he learned, how God changed his life this week, why he is thankful, etc.). Here the evangelist makes his last call for God, giving each camper one final opportunity to step forward for the Lord.

DON'T TAKE A VACATION FROM GOD!

CHAMBERS CHILDREN'S CAMP
WESLEYAN METHODIST

You notice that most of the adults in the church are jumpy and at least slightly overweight. That's not going to happen to you. Yet you sit down one morning, pour a cup of coffee, and force yourself to drink the vile stuff. You do this four days in a row. By the fifth morning you look forward to the private ritual, and you can't wait for the chance to show the adults at church that you are now capable of engaging in fellowship.

As central to the faith as this fellowship is, on Sundays it takes place only on a private basis. You might be invited to someone else's home for Sunday dinner or for dessert after the evening service, but on Sunday no food or coffee is served in the church.

Be Present at Our Table, Lord: Food and the Believer

* What a Fellowship *

Real Christians like to fellowship, and they find it hard to do this unless they have something to put into their mouths while they give the other person a chance to say something. Since this can't be cigarettes, it is food—or coffee. You wonder what would happen to the world economy if real Christians had convictions against caffeine. The Women's Christian Temperance Union must have known there is only so much you can ask; if people will give up alcohol, let them drink as much coffee and eat as much food as they like.

Pastor Lee Comes to Dinner

An after-church coffee hour is a sure sign of a liberal church; they may know the importance of fellowship, but they have no respect for the Lord's Day.

On Sunday mornings the church basement is divided into six small, dark classrooms. But on Friday night it's one big hall, lined with tables set end to end and covered with a white paper tablecloth that you're sure would be a block long if you unwound the roll in the middle of the street. On Friday nights the smell of food and coffee overpowers the usual smell of mildew.

One by one the ample women clomp down the stairs and proudly set their quickly cooling foil-covered offerings on the counter separating the kitchen from the large room. You want to peek under the foil, but you wait. You notice, though, that the woman in charge of the food committee uncovers a corner of every dish for a quick look—always on the inhale. Tonight they are fortunate. Only two offerings of Spanish rice and only one baked beans.

You and your friends wait close but not too close to the food lineup. You don't have to be the first in line, but you feel sorry for the women on the food committee who have to stand back and eat after everyone else has gone through. The pastor thanks God for the hands of the women who prepared the food, and then you pile it up on your white paper

plate. It's hard to take a little bit of everything without getting the flavors mixed up. You know it all gets mixed up in your stomach, but you can't stand for it to happen before it gets there. You eat until you can't possibly get another thing in—except a square piece of chocolate cake, which has arrived in abundance.

This is so much better than eating at home. Why can't they have church suppers every week?

Be present at our table, Lord;
Be here and everywhere adored.
These mercies bless, and grant that we
May eat and drink and live for Thee.
(Sung to tune of the "Doxology")
—Traditional

✳ The Sunday School Picnic ✳

Imagination not required! Sunday School Picnics don't need fancy names or fancy foods. Simple fare, prepared by loving hands.

If you attend the Sunday School Picnic, you should bring your own plate and silverware and one of the following:

> Potato salad
> Macaroni salad
> Cole slaw
> Relish tray
> Potato chips
> Deviled eggs
> Baked beans
> Red Jell-O filled with fruit and covered with
>   miniature marshmallows

Families with four or more attending should also bring a dessert. Any one of the following is appropriate:

> Chocolate cake
> Apple pie
> Chocolate chip cookies
> Watermelon
> Red Jell-O filled with fruit and covered with
>   miniature marshmallows

The Sunday School will provide:

> Hot dogs and buns
> Hamburgers and buns
> Coffee, iced tea, Kool-Aid
> Ice cream cups (packed in dry ice)

Activities for a Sunday School Picnic may include:

Potato sack races

Three-legged races

Wheelbarrow races

Relay races

Peanut hunt

Tug-of-war

Water balloon fight

Softball

Volleyball

Drop the clothespins into the milk bottle

Watermelon-eating contest

✳ The Church Supper ✳

Also known as Covered Dish Supper, Hotdish Supper, Potluck Dinner, or Potfaith Dinner. Limited imagination permitted. After all, this meal includes hot food as well.

Bring your own flatware plus one of the following:

Spanish rice

Tuna noodle casserole

Scalloped potatoes

Fried chicken

Baked beans

Spanish rice

Meat loaf

Green bean, mushroom soup, and
    french-fried-onion casserole

Macaroni and cheese

Spanish rice

Lasagna

Five-cup salad

Applesauce

Red Jell-O filled with fruit and
    covered with miniature
    marshmallows

Carrot-and-raisin salad

Deviled eggs

Spanish rice

Families with four or more in attendance should also bring a dessert. Try any of the following:

Chocolate cake

Apple pie

Banana cupcakes

Chocolate chip cookies

Red Jell-O filled with fruit and covered with miniature marshmallows

The church will supply rolls, coffee, tea, and Kool-Aid.

Red Jello Filled with Fruit
and Covered w/ Miniature Marshmellows

1 6 oz box Jello (cherry, raspberry, or strawberry)
1 cup boiling water
1-2 cups fruit (fruit cocktail, peaches, pears, strawberries, bananas, raspberries) If canned, drain, reserving liquid. If frozen, thaw and drain, reserving liquid.
In a medium sizzered Tupperware bowl (one w/a lid), mix together Jello and boiling water, stirring until Jello dissolves. Add enough cold water to fruit liquid to make 1 cup liquid. Stir into Jello mixture. Allow to cool until Jello is partially set. Stir in fruit, mixing well. Sprinkle with miniature marshmellows and bits of fruit. Place in frig until firmly set.

✴ I Would Be True ✴

Food is also the foundation of the church's local charity. The women of the church are asked to provide ample quantities of food in the following situations:

When a member of a church family dies. You are to take casseroles and cakes to the house as soon as you get word of the death. After the funeral you are to help put on a dinner for the family and for anyone who drove more than forty miles to pay respects.

When a church daughter marries. You are to sign up to bring a portion of the wedding reception meal which is served in the church basement.

When any woman of the church is hospitalized. Someday it could be you, and if it were, you'd fear for the quality of food your husband would serve your children. In hopes that the bread you cast on the waters will be returned to you, you always send a casserole when another woman gets sick.

At Harvest Home. This yearly autumn food collection is taken as a thank-you offering for the pastor's family. From the back of your pantry shelf you pull a can of spinach that's been there so long it's starting to rust. You also buy a five-pound bag of flour and slip both into the box on your way into church.

At Christmas. For the shut-ins you fill baskets with fruit and nonperishable food items. If the pastor or a pushy layman insists, you might also collect canned and dry goods for the Rescue Mission or the Salvation Army to distribute. You contribute to this project, but halfheartedly. You feel it's more important to take care of one's own than to take care of strangers who are outside the fold.

Foods We Do Best

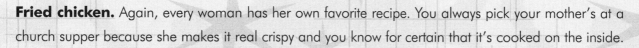

Meat loaf. Every lady has her own favorite recipe. The actual loaf itself doesn't matter as long as there's enough ketchup smeared all over the top.

Fried chicken. Again, every woman has her own favorite recipe. You always pick your mother's at a church supper because she makes it real crispy and you know for certain that it's cooked on the inside.

Scalloped potatoes and ham. No church supper would be complete without at least one offering of scalloped potatoes in which the potatoes are not cooked all the way through. Nothing beats the crunch of uncooked scalloped potatoes.

Spanish rice. What is Spanish about Spanish rice? And why do so many people bring it to church suppers?

Baked beans. Take two big cans of Campbell's Baked Beans, add some ketchup, some brown sugar, maybe a few onions. Lay strips of bacon across the top and bake until done.

Deviled eggs. How is it that folks who are so meticulous about their vocabulary would permit something called deviled eggs at a church function? Or devil's food cake for that matter?

Potato salad. One of those dishes that somehow brings out the creative side of people. You often end up with really bizarre ingredients in what should be simple summer fare. We recommend that you always look closely before eating it.

Tuna noodle casserole. Who invented this?

Lemonade. Real lemonade, not that fake stuff you get today. This is the kind with the seeds at the bottom of the pitcher and slices of lemon floating among the ice cubes. And lots of sugar!

Chapter Six

The Church's One Foundation

The Church's One Foundation

Doctrine: those teachings that ultimately separate the men from the boys. Or in this case, the saved from the unsaved, the redeemed from the lost. We have no formal catechism, no doctrine classes, no articles of faith. We learn the principles of our faith from our parents and from our Sunday School teachers, through sermons, Bible stories, Sunday School lessons, daily devotion books, Aunt Theresa, and Danny Orlis.

We quickly learned the cues that introduce doctrinal teaching: "We believe. . . ." "Real Christians. . . ." "The Bible teaches. . . ." "God says. . . ." When we heard these phrases we knew that what followed were beliefs essential to our faith. And it is important always to remember that *all* doctrine and *all* teaching are based not on what men say but on what the Bible says. For there is no question in life that is not answered in Scripture.

Fundamental to all teaching is that we are different, separate from all others. "Come out from among them and be ye separate." "Be not conformed to this world." "Ye have not chosen me, but I have chosen you." We are not like the world; we are not even like other people who *say* they are Christians. Our practices are meant to distinguish us from all others. We learn that we will never fit in, never belong. We are different. We are set apart. We are real Christians.

These distinctions are most apparent in the way we celebrate Communion, in our method of baptism, in how we view Sin and the World, and in our expectations for the End of the World.

Break Thou the Bread of Life: *Communion*

We never really know why, but it doesn't happen every Sunday. In fact, it comes around so seldom that it catches you by surprise every time.

You can tell as soon as you walk into the sanctuary with your parents after Sunday School that this is it. The wooden table at the front inscribed with *This Do in Remembrance of Me* is draped with a large white cloth. It's Communion Sunday.

Church lasts longer when it's Communion Sunday. You always hope the pastor will preach shorter—and he never does. But throughout his unabbreviated sermon, the sense of expectation is heightened by the array of bumps and bulges beneath the cloth, as well as by the presence of two rows of dark-suited men at the front of the church.

At the appropriate time—after the hymns, the offertory, and the sermon, when your hunger pangs are just beginning in earnest—the men go up and lift the cloth from the Communion table, revealing gleaming silver platters stocked with crackers and grape juice. They fold the cloth while the pastor comes down from his "throne" on the elevated platform and reads from the large black Bible draped in a ministerial way over his left hand. (The covers of your own Bible are stiff, but ministers' Bibles are specially designed for pliability and an easy drape.)

"For I have received from the Lord that which also I delivered unto you," he intones, "that the Lord Jesus, the same night in which he was betrayed, took bread. . . ."

It isn't bread, exactly—it's tiny white squares. You remember them from last time, smaller than soda crackers, with a dot in the center of each square. They taste like absolutely nothing. (Other churches cut up slices of Wonder Bread into tiny cubes. Some even use matzos!)

"Please hold the elements until everyone is served," the pastor is reminding everyone, "and we will all partake together."

Now the organ begins to play "Break Thou the Bread of Life" as the dark-suited men—some of whom you recognize as the fathers of kids in Sunday School—move into action. Each one carries a large silver platter as they fan out across the sanctuary. (You have tried in vain to guess where each one will go.) Two of them move up your section, passing platters back and forth across the rows.

When at last they arrive at your row, your dad on the aisle seat holds the heavy platter for you as you select a square. Then he reaches over and hands it to your mother on the other side. The square in your fingers feels smooth, cool. *This is Jesus' body.*

Finally the men are grouped up front and the organ stops. The pastor prays a prayer, then says: "When Jesus had given thanks, he brake it, and said, 'Take, eat; this is my body, which is broken for you: this do in remembrance of me.'"

After a split-second pause everyone's hand moves toward his or her mouth. You join in the solemn ritual, slipping the square into your mouth, feeling a rush of saliva, and straining to hear crunches around you.

You are still holding your square on your tongue when the pastor continues, "In the same manner also he took the cup." The men again fan out, this time carrying gleaming silver trays rattling with tiny glasses of grape juice. The organ begins to play "There Is a Fountain Filled with Blood."

It seems forever till the men arrive at your row and your father holds the tray in front of you. You select the fullest glass you see and stare fascinated at the tiny glass of purple liquid after the tray moves on, concentrating on keeping it as steady as you can. You worry that if you don't keep an eye on it, it will tilt slightly or swivel in your hand

and spill onto your lap. You also wonder, will it take one swallow or two to empty the glass? If there's a little bit left when you thought you'd finished, won't everyone see you tip your head back and drink again?

At last the organ stops and the pastor prays a brief prayer. This creates a conflict, since you need to keep an eye on your glass, so you squeeze your eyes open periodically to keep watch. Finally he concludes, "Jesus said, 'This cup is the new testament in my blood: this do ye, as oft as ye drink it, in remembrance of me.'"

Everyone's head tips back to drink, and you discover when you lower your cup that you have indeed finished it all. A little purple is collecting at the bottom, which your tongue could clean out. Could your tongue fit in there?

The grown-ups are already slipping their cups

into the wooden holders in the pews in front of them. You put your glass there, too, wondering who comes around to collect and wash them.

The army of men at the front is unfolding the white cloth and draping it once again over the table. Do these men take so much trouble folding blankets or tea towels at home?

Next week the wooden table at the front will be clear, the trays and cloth gone, and the dark-suited men sitting with their families. Communion Sunday is over.

Just then, as if to compete with the choral postlude, your stomach growls ominously. Obviously it's past time for dinner.

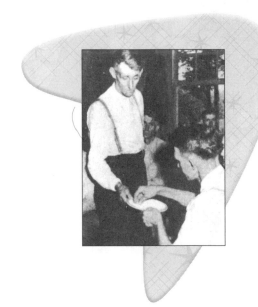

Born Again Lingo

Backslide: Be saved, then fall back into old, worldly habits.

Rededicate Your Life: If you backslide, you can repent of your ways and go forward to rededicate your life. There are no limits to how many times you can rededicate your life. Some folks with tender consciences may do it many times over the course of a year.

Under Conviction: A situation in which a person senses that God is asking him to make a decision or rebuking him for sin. It is an indication of unfinished business. Closely related to the feeling you get when you haven't visited your mother for a month, and when you do, she tells you that she's been sick ("It's really nothing"), that nobody's been to see her ("It's not so bad; I got caught up on my housework"), and she heard about your promotion from your Aunt Rose ("You have time to talk to her!"). You feel (or you should feel) under conviction. It's a lot like feeling guilty.

✳ There Is a Fountain: Baptism ✳

The need to be baptized dawns on you slowly. You were saved two years ago. You develop a new spiritual awareness, a new sense of right and wrong. You are intent on loving God and being the sort of person He likes to have around.

Then gradually you realize that you need to take another important step in your spiritual journey. Baptism. You may witness a baptismal service in your church. Your parents may suggest that you should consider such a step. The pastor may challenge you to make a public commitment of faith. However the realization comes, you find yourself moving inexorably toward this new step.

Baptism is the most marvelously dramatic ceremony in the born again church. All that water!

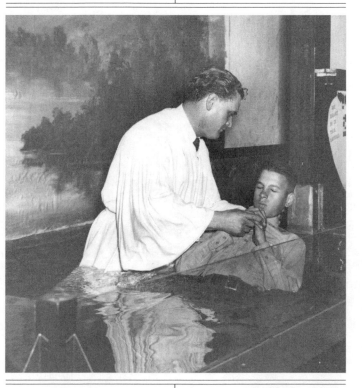

Grown-ups plunging into the water fully clothed. Your pastor, of all adults most distinguished and honored, standing up to his waist in a pool of water wearing a suit. Without giggle or embarrassment! Baptism truly defies every notion of sensible behavior.

When you hesitantly bring up the subject with your parents, you see them exchange Significant Glances. Your mother asks, "Why do you want to be baptized?" You shrug your shoulders. "Because I'm saved." And so begins your preparation for this grand public confession of faith.

Baptism, you learn, is the public step by which you make your private commitment to Jesus known to the church. It is the step that finalizes and formalizes your salvation. *No*, it doesn't save you. And no, not being baptized won't keep you out of Heaven. But it does show that you are courageous enough to stand up for Jesus.

Total Immersion is the only kind of baptism that takes. Sprinkling doesn't count. After all, Jesus was immersed. And the New Testament speaks of going down *into* the water for baptism.

As the big day comes closer, you begin to feel quivery inside. Has anyone ever drowned while being baptized? One Sunday the pastor keeps all the baptismal candidates after church. You are given a paper that explains what you should wear. The pastor tells you that you should bring towels, a change of clothes, and a white handkerchief. He then shows you what is going to happen: how to hold on, how to position your feet so they hold you when you come up out of the water. He makes reassuring little jokes about how he's never lost anyone yet. (Heh, heh.)

Some churches are large enough to have a baptistry of their own. It isn't something that looks like a fancy birdbath, either. Usually it is a small pool nestled behind (or even hidden *underneath*) the choir loft. Small churches will either borrow one (use a larger church's facilities off-hours) or use a pond or lake. Currently, the Pacific Ocean, Beverly Hills swimming pools, and hot tubs are considered vogue.

When the big day arrives, you wonder if Jesus would understand if you changed your mind. After a little thought, you know that He would understand, but no one else would. You don't eat breakfast. (Don't want to risk cramps.) You wear semi-good clothes. You pack your overnight bag with all your post-baptismal needs.

This is one time you don't have to sit through the service. After you drop off your bag in the dressing room (really the pastor's study), you join the other candidates in the waiting area. You peek through the door to the sanctuary. The church is packed; all your friends are sitting in the front row to see if they can make you laugh.

As the ceremony begins, the pastor slowly sloshes into the pool,

his Bible held high. He turns to face the congregation which sits awed into complete silence by the vision of this man in a suit speaking from the pool. He reads from his Bible the story of John baptizing Jesus.

As the youngest, you are first. You take a deep breath and begin your walk into the water toward his outstretched arms. The water is so cold you let out a gasp. He stands you sideways between him and the congregation and asks, "Have you accepted Jesus Christ as your personal Savior?" You reply loudly enough that everyone can hear, "Yes I have."

"I then baptize you in the name of the Father, and the Son, and the Holy Ghost."

He takes your handkerchief, places it over your face, and puts his other hand behind your neck. As you hold on to his arm with both hands, he leans you

backwards into the water until you are completely submerged. Totally covered, thoroughly soaked.

He then brings you back through the swirling waters. You stand up, the water sucking and grabbing at your hair and clothes. As you regain your balance and try not to choke, you move toward the exit side of the pool, toward comforting arms, dry towels, and encouraging hugs.

You have been baptized.

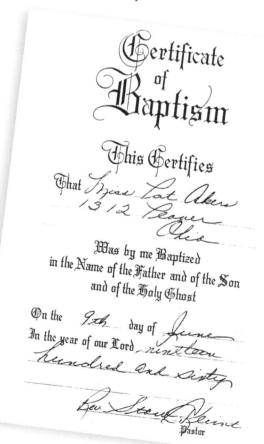

Ten Things to Worry about Regarding Baptism

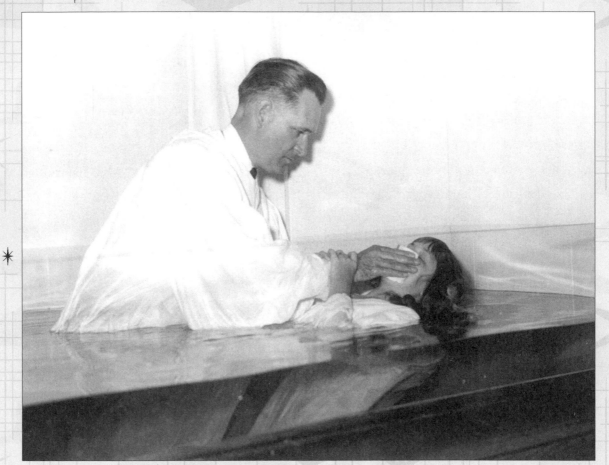

1 What if I drown?

2 What if the pastor drops me and I hit my head on the bottom of the baptistry?

3 What if the pastor's son told him that I snickered during last week's sermon and he holds my head under the water for an extra long time?

4 What if I forget to hold my nose and come up sputtering and everyone starts laughing?

5 What if Wally Krenslow gets baptized before me and his Brylcreem makes the water greasy?

6 What if, after the baptism, when I'm ready to go up the stairs out of the baptistry, I slip and fall back into the water?

7 What if my clothes are so wet and heavy that they fall off as I start to leave the baptistry and everyone sees my underwear . . . or worse?

8 What if the pastor saw me trying to cut into line at the Sunday School picnic, so when my turn comes he refuses to baptize me?

9 What if Susie Thompson jumps up when it's my turn and tells everyone that she saw me eating M&M's in church and then the pastor refuses to baptize me?

10 What if I drown?

Make Me a Blessing: The World

The World is a very dangerous place. The World represents all things temporal, pleasure-seeking, self-serving, and ungodly.

When you *love the World,* your priorities are on things that are not eternal, not of God.

If you care more about things like clothes and dates and cars than you do about God, then you are *worldly.*

The condition of putting money and social position and career before God is *worldliness.*

Difficulties come when *worldly* becomes more of a descriptive term. Say you consider baking a cake on Sunday to be work, but your friend Joyce considers it affordable recreation. Since the Bible doesn't identify this activity as *sin,* you are forced to decry it as *worldly. Worldly* is the next best thing to sin.

Thus *worldly* can be a very useful term, since it can be used to describe anyone who disagrees with your views or enjoys any activity from which you abstain. You will also find, if applied to you, that it is impossible to argue successfully in your own defense. The minute you try to explain why you aren't worldly, you are plunged into a "Who Really Knows God Best" contest, with self-righteousness as the first prize.

Most folks eventually discover that the best policy is to focus on God's opinion of their own lives. And once they start, they find it keeps them pretty busy.

✳ The Communists Are Coming ✳

There's no doubt about it. The Communists are coming, and soon. You are as sure of this as you are of the Second Coming, but the time frame is not exactly clear to you and you pray that Jesus will come first. Why? Because the Communists, which is to say the Russians, are going to torture you and imprison you for being a Christian. This thought gives you nightmares, yet you're ready to stand up and be counted. The Communists are ready to die for their cause and you are ready to die for yours. You remember the compelling line: "If it were against the law to be a Christian, would there be enough evidence to convict you?" You surely hope so. With thrilling dread, you imagine yourself in prison.

But you've heard conflicting stories. Some seem to say that the Russians aren't going to need much evidence of faith. They have a list—the names and addresses of every member of every Bible-believing church in America. And they're just going to come and knock on your door. Of course they'll have a great advantage over you because they can all speak English but you can't speak Russian. You should be trying to learn it now so you'll be ahead of everyone else. You're all going to have to speak it eventually; that is, if the desk you climb under does save you from the bomb the Russians are going to drop on your school. At least you'll have a little warning because you don't live in Wheaton, Illinois, or Wilmore, Kentucky, which are the Russians' first targets. But then just maybe Jesus will come before the Communists. What if it were today?

Questions We've Always Wanted to Ask Catholics

How do you know when to stand up and sit down in the church service?

Why can't you wear a rosary around your neck like a necklace?

How do you know what to confess at confession?

What makes Holy Water holy?

Do nuns have hair?

What do priests wear under their robes?

Why aren't you allowed to read the Bible?

What is Purgatory?

What is Limbo?

What does it mean to buy pagan babies?

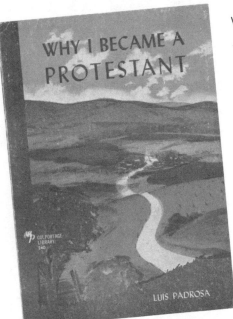

WHY I BECAME A PROTESTANT

LUIS PADROSA

A Shorter Catechism

Miracles: We believe that miracles stopped at the end of the New Testament. Miracles are something those folks needed in order to believe. But God stopped doing miracles after that. We don't need miracles because we have the Bible.

Tongues: We don't believe in tongues. That is something they just did in the New Testament. But once they finished writing the New Testament, they stopped speaking in tongues. So we don't speak in tongues.

Saints: Anyone who has accepted Jesus as personal Savior is a saint. We don't call anyone Saint So-and-So. We don't believe that you can pray to saints or that they protect you.

Halos: We never send out Christmas cards that picture anyone but Jesus with a halo. Except maybe angels. Angels can have halos.

Printed prayers: We don't use prayers that are printed out on paper or in a book. We believe that anyone who is a real Christian can pray to God in his or her own words.

The Judgment Test

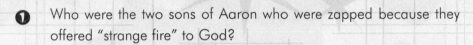

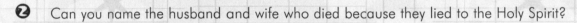

Growing up born again, you knew that God is a God of justice as well as a God of love. You may have worried about it a little . . . you may still worry. Test your own Fear of God Quotient by seeing if you know the answers to the following questions:

❶ Who were the two sons of Aaron who were zapped because they offered "strange fire" to God?

❷ Can you name the husband and wife who died because they lied to the Holy Spirit?

❸ Who was eaten by worms because he accepted the praise of people who said he spoke "like a god"?

❹ Whose kingdom was taken away from him because he failed to kill all of the Amalekites as God commanded?

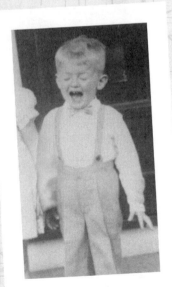

❺ Name the prophet who was killed by a lion because he disobeyed God's command to return home immediately after delivering his prophetic message.

❻ Can you name the man who died because he touched the Ark of the Covenant to keep it from falling?

❼ Whose wife turned into a pillar of salt because she looked back to see her hometown being destroyed by fire from heaven?

❽ Who was not allowed to enter the promised land because he struck a rock instead of speaking to it?

❾ Name the prophet whose curse caused 42 children to be killed by bears after they called him "baldy." (The children called him "baldy," not the bears.)

Answers: ❶ Nadab and Abihu; ❷ Ananias and Sapphira; ❸ King Herod; ❹ Saul; ❺ A "man of God," we don't know his name; ❻ Uzza; ❼ Lot's wife; ❽ Moses; ❾ Elisha

Give yourself 10 points for every correct answer. If you scored anything less than 80, you need to remember that the fear of the Lord is the beginning of wisdom!

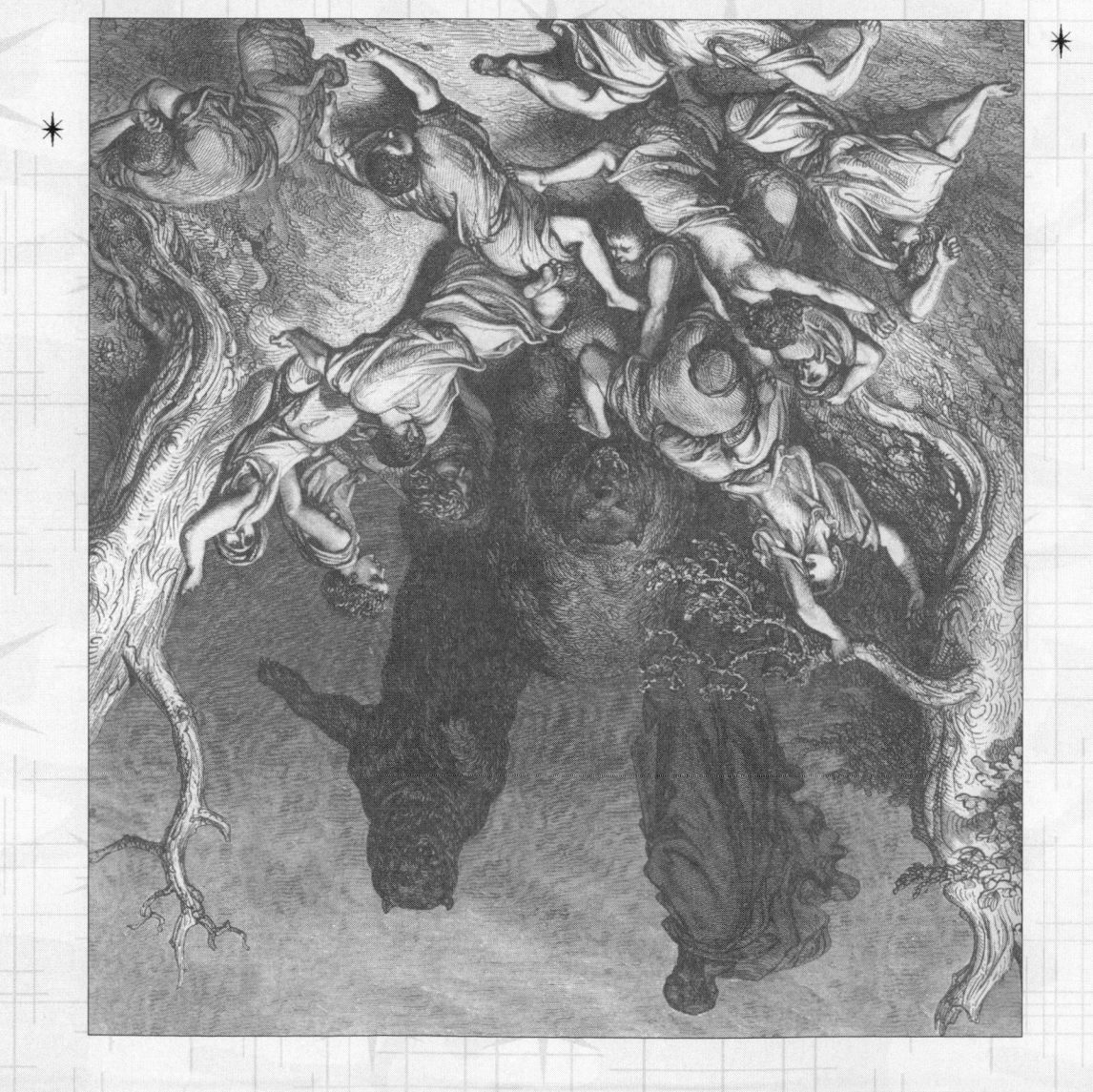

What If It Were Today?
* The End Times *

Most born-againers, at some point or other in their lives, encounter The Chart. Your pastor may spend an entire year of Sunday evenings teaching it. You may take a Moody Extension Course on eschatology. Or your dad may have a Chart in his Bible that he uses for his personal Bible study.

The Chart is, of course, the outline of Dispensationalism, which is God's plan for mankind. It shows the big picture, how history and the future all fit together.

The Chart provides a sense of belonging, a sense that God is in charge, that there is a plan. There is enormous relief in seeing just how organized everything really is.

As you can see, there are seven dispensations

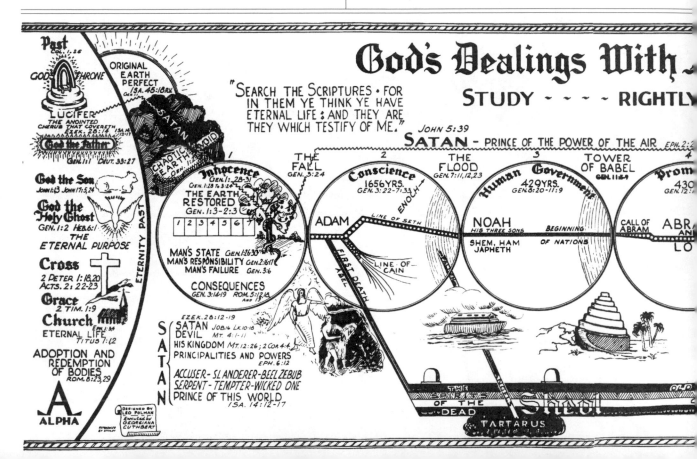

(or key historical periods). Each dispensation represents a separate period of time during which God established different requirements for his relationships with people.

The best part of this chart is the little drawings showing everything that happens during a particular dispensation. You can sit for hours just gazing at the pictures.

In all fairness, not all born-againers subscribe to Dispensationalism. Some believe in Covenant Theology, which says that there is a continuity to God's relationships with men. The relationship doesn't change depending on what period of history you're in. Too bad they don't have charts. It would certainly be more fun to learn about it if they did.

If you have any questions after studying The Chart, you may want to read *The Late Great Planet Earth,* which is The Chart turned best-seller.

* * *

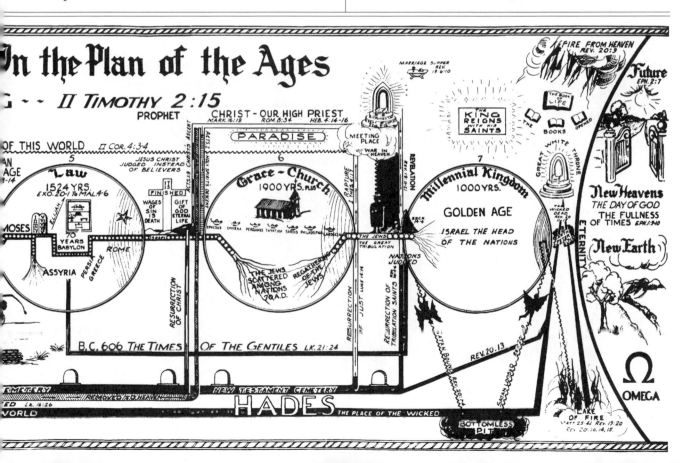

112 The Meeting in the Air.

A. A. P.   D. B. TOWNER.

1. How it thrills our hearts with rapt-u:e As we feel the hour is nigh,
2. Oft the wea - ry miles di - vide us From the friends we cher-ish so,
3. O the hope of His ap - pear - ing—How it lights the drear-y way,

When the voice of the arch - an - gel Shall re - sound through-out the sky,
And the look from eyes that love us—How we miss wher-e'er we go!
How it girds our souls with cour-age For the "lit - tle while" we stay!

And the dead in Christ, up-springing, With the liv - ing saints shall be
And some-times the grave has hid - den One whose face was ver - y dear—
For it can - not be much long-er Till the Bride-groom calls us home:

Caught a - way from all earth's shad-ows To a glad e - ter - ni - ty!
O what joy once more to meet them When the Mas - ter shall ap - pear!
Sure - ly, sure - ly He comes quick-ly! E - ven so, Lord Je - sus, come!

CHORUS.

O the meet-ing in the air! O the meet-ing in the air,

Copyright, 1906, by Daniel B. Towner. English copyright.

Antichrist: The evil, earthly ruler whose rise to power will signal the Last Days and the Second Coming of Christ. Also called "the Beast."

Last Days: The time just preceding the Second Coming of Christ.

Millennium: The thousand-year period when Christ shall reign on earth and Satan will be stripped of his powers. Everyone will be happy and there will be no more problems.

Rapture: The transference of Christians from earth into the presence of Christ. The key question is when the Rapture will occur. If you believe in a Post-Tribulation Rapture, you believe that the Rapture will occur at the end of the Tribulation (meaning you will go through the great persecution). Most born again folk subscribe to a Pre-Tribulation Rapture position: The Rapture will occur before the Tribulation begins, exempting you from the persecution. Although there is solace in believing you will not face persecution, you can't help but wonder if facing persecution might after all be the real test of Christian character. Anyway, what are all those raptured folks going to do for seven years? Will they be processed?

Tribulation: Seven years of persecution and bad times during which the Antichrist will rule. Often called the Last Days.

✴ The Rapture ✴

What Is It?

Jesus is coming back someday, and all the Christians, dead and alive, will meet Him in the air.

How Will It Happen?

You remember the flannel-graph story about the Rapture. There will be a shout of the archangel and a trumpet blast. The dead in Christ will rise first. Then Christians who are alive will be caught up, together, to meet Jesus in a cloud.

It will be very fast—"in the twinkling of an eye." No one has ever clocked the twinkling of an eye, but it is even faster than a wink or a blink. There will be no time to accept Jesus as your Savior at the last minute, as bodies whoosh into the sky like metal filings to a magnet.

It will be totally unexpected. Only God the Father knows exactly

when—not even Jesus knows. Ignore any full-page ads in the *New York Times* announcing the date in advance. Likewise, give gurus with timetables a wide berth.

It will probably *not* happen at night. Too many people are expecting that, since the Bible says Jesus will come like "a thief in the night."

When Will It Happen?

Some Christians are pre-Trib: They think the Rapture will happen before the Tribulation. These are the same people who wear polyester leisure suits.

Some Christians are post-Trib: They think it will happen after the Tribulation. Their cellar walls are stacked with canned goods and bottled water, and they can give you exact directions to all the municipal fallout shelters within a fifty-mile radius. The most radical stock guns and ammunition in their cellars, too.

Some Christians are mid-Trib: They're sympathetic to the pre-Tribbers but their gut feeling is that the post-Tribbers are right.

For further information about the Rapture, be sure to see the film *A Thief in the Night*.

* Eternity *

If you were to move all the beaches of the world one grain of sand at a time, by the time you'd moved them all, Eternity would just be beginning.

If a bird brushed his tail against the tip of a mountain once every thousand years, by the time he'd rubbed that mountain down to nothing, Eternity would just be beginning.

Opportune and Inopportune

It would be *bad* to be raptured:

. . . before Aunt Connie and Uncle Bill get saved.

. . . before you get your driver's permit.

. . . before you lose your baby fat, get the braces off your teeth, buy contact lenses, peroxide your hair, and wear makeup so both you and your friends can see what you really look like!

. . . before your first kiss.

. . . before summer vacation ends.

. . . before your wedding day.

. . . before your wedding night.

. . . before you make up after a big fight with your _____ (best friend, boyfriend, girlfriend, parents, boss, etc.).

Moments for the Rapture

It would be *good* to be raptured:

. . . before the Tribulation.

. . . before sixth period and Miss Crocket's chemistry exam.

. . . before the dentist drills your teeth again.

. . . before the match ignites the sticks stacked up to your neck if you're martyred for the faith.

. . . before your dad discovers the dent you put in his new Chevrolet.

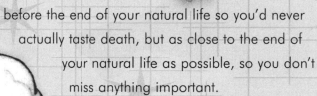

. . . before the end of your natural life so you'd never actually taste death, but as close to the end of your natural life as possible, so you don't miss anything important.

Chapter Seven

There's Within My Heart a Melody

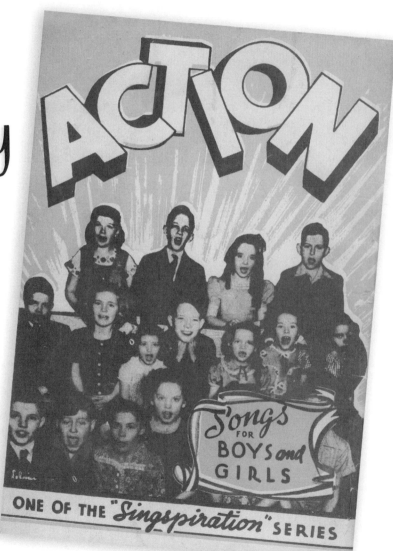

There's Within My Heart a Melody

The Melody Lingers On ...

You know you grew up born again when you:

* find yourself praying for a parking space.

* find yourself praying for the good guys in a movie. (Hey, what are you doing at the movies?)

* resist walking into a highly recommended café because of the neon beer sign in the window.

* make obscure Bible references at work, then suddenly realize that no one knows what you're talking about.

* continue to find words like *tribulation* and *lasciviousness* and *burden* creeping into your vocabulary.

* come home to an empty house and wonder if the Rapture took place and you were left behind.

* still check your car radio before anyone gets into the car, to make sure it's not set to a station that plays the wrong kind of music.

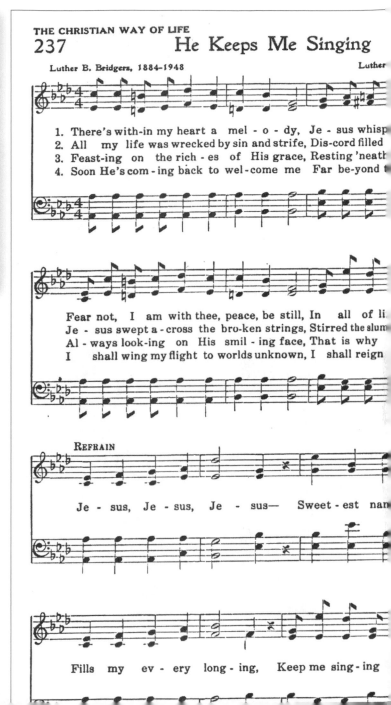

THE CHRISTIAN WAY OF LIFE
237   He Keeps Me Singing

Luther B. Bridgers, 1884-1948   Luther

1. There's with-in my heart a mel - o - dy, Je - sus whisp
2. All my life was wrecked by sin and strife, Dis-cord filled
3. Feast-ing on the rich - es of His grace, Resting 'neath
4. Soon He's com - ing back to wel-come me Far be-yond t

Fear not, I am with thee, peace, be still, In all of li
Je - sus swept a - cross the bro-ken strings, Stirred the slum
Al - ways look-ing on His smil - ing face, That is why
I shall wing my flight to worlds unknown, I shall reign

REFRAIN

Je - sus, Je - sus, Je - sus— Sweet - est nam

Fills my ev - ery long - ing, Keep me sing-ing

✳ The Semifinal Judgment ✳

No, this is not the Judgment Seat of Christ or the Great White Throne Judgment. This is simply a short review to see how much you really learned about the born again world.

1 Your youth group is trying to plan the next social. The most important question to be answered is:

a. Where can we hold a dance?

b. What movie should we see?

c. What'll we eat?

2 To raise some money for their Missionary Emergency Fund, the Missionary Ladies Circle decides to:

a. hold a Bake Sale at the local shopping center.

b. request that the deacons take a special offering.

c. sponsor a Las Vegas Night in the church hall.

d. have a kissing booth in the church vestibule on the last Sunday of every month.

❸ Your father asks you to put some nice music on the hi-fi. Your selection includes:

a. Perry Como's "We Get Letters," West Side Story Original Cast Album, "Liberace at the Piano," and Peggy Lee's "Lover."

b. Bill Haley and the Comets, Elvis Presley, the Everly Brothers, and Pat Boone.

c. "Les Barnett Plays the Hymns of Fanny Crosby," The Haven of Rest Quartet's "Shipmates of Song," Thurlow Spurr and the Spurrlows' "Pages From the Old Hymnbook," and Bill Pearce and Dick Anthony's "Over the Sunset Mountains."

❹ You walk into a room and on the table you see an overturned box of alphabet macaroni, a pile of Popsicle sticks, four half-filled jars of glitter, scraps of felt, six miniature bottles of Elmer's Glue, and two stunned women with red and blue glitter in their hair. You realize immediately that:

a. you are in the Art Therapy Room at the state hospital.

b. punk rock has found its way to middle America.

c. the handicrafts session at Vacation Bible School has just ended.

❼ How did Moses cross the Red Sea?

  a. Did he swim?

  b. Did he sail?

  c. Did he fly?

  d. Did he walk?

  e. Did he run?

  f. God blew with His wind

      (puff, puff, puff, puff)

    Blew just enough

      ('nuf, 'nuf, 'nuf, 'nuf)

    And through the sea God made a path.

❺ Girls should always wear dresses that modestly cover their knees because:

  a. to boys, knees look like breasts.

  b. short skirts make a girl look cheap.

  c. a good Christian girl knows that inner spiritual beauty is more important than outer, worldly beauty.

  d. all of the above.

❻ Born again kids never learn ballet, tap dancing, or baton twirling because:

  a. you don't need those skills on the mission field.

  b. sequins are unscriptural.

  c. you can't use them in the annual Christmas pageant (the showcase for born again performing arts).

  d. they are worldly activities.

Answers: **❶** c. The most important question at any born again function is "What'll we eat?" The born again church has made recreational eating an art form. **❷** b. Born again folks are not at all comfortable with the idea of getting something in return for a gift. When you give to the church, you should be giving to God, so the gift should come from a grateful heart. But this is beginning to change; note the current fund-raising techniques offering a free book or tape in return for a donation. **❸** c. None of those other records would even be in the house! **❹** c. **❺** d. Really! That's what the camp counselor told us. (The same one who used to undress in the closet.) **❻** d. Actually all of the answers have some truth to them, but d is what we were told. **❼** f. "That's how he got across." If you'd been in Sunday School, you would have known this, too.

Conclusion

And so our nostalgic journey comes to a close. Remembering the details—the trivial and the nonessential as well as the important foundational basics—of our early years has helped us see just how much we have in common, though we grew up in different homes and attended different churches in different parts of the country. We can laugh at our peculiarities, acknowledge our failings, and gratefully appreciate why we are the way we are.

The exercise of remembering our roots—the forms and rituals of our childhood faith—also brought us to a deeper understanding and appreciation of our present-tense faith: It lives. It is essential and vital, and because it lives, we encourage you to seek the living Lord, whose mercy is everlasting.

Patricia Klein was born in Akron, Ohio, in 1949. At age five she gave her first (and last) solo performance, singing "I'll Be a Sunbeam for Jesus" in front of the entire Sunday School. This marked the start of a childhood dedicated to Bible camp, youth group, and daily Vacation Bible School. After graduating from Moody Bible Institute (the "West Point of Christian Service") in 1970, she moved to San Francisco, then to New York, where she pursued a life in books, both selling them and creating them. She is the author of *Worship Without Words: The Signs and Symbols of Our Faith* (Paraclete Press) and lives in Fairfax, Virginia.

Jane Campbell (born in Oak Park, Illinois, in 1951) grew up in Wheaton, Illinois, and Houghton, New York, and had the great fortune at age four to meet the beloved radio storyteller Aunt Theresa. At age five she recited Psalm 23 with her brother on WMBI radio; at seven she won an 1884 silver dollar for memorizing Hebrews 1; at eight she joined Jet Cadets by reciting 1 Corinthians 13; and at nine she gave her first public testimony. Formerly managing editor of *Christian Herald*, she has been with Chosen Books (currently as editorial director) since 1978 and lives with a dog and three born-again cats in Fairfax, Virginia.

David Wimbish was born in Mesa, Arizona, in 1949. One of his earliest childhood memories is the time he recited Psalm 23 in front of the congregation: "He maketh me to lie down in green plaster." He also vividly recalls the Sunday morning when he was twelve that his pants fell down in church. David's grandfather, father, uncle, and eldest brother were all preachers, proving that preachers' kids do turn out right. He attended Pepperdine University and graduated from Northern Arizona University with a B.S. in journalism. He is currently creative supervisor for the Russ Reid Company, an advertising agency in Pasadena, and has written or cowritten more than thirty books.

Evelyn Bence was born in Rochester, New York. Her father was a preacher and, as they say, once a preacher's kid, always a preacher's kid. In 1974 she graduated from Houghton College where she learned to separate the men from the boys. Although her B.A. was in business administration, she grew disenchanted with figures and intrigued with words. She's the author of several books, including *Spiritual Moments with the Great Hymns*. Her life verse is Hebrews 11:13, "They admitted they were aliens and strangers on earth." She currently resides in Virginia, where she works as a self-employed editor and writer.

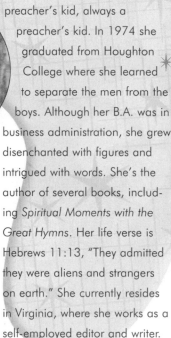

Laura Pearson was born in 1950 in Wheaton, Illinois, where she spent many happy hours (with Jane) playing freeze tag and king-of-the-mountain on the front lawn of Wheaton College, a school she later attended and graduated from with a B.A. in Spanish and economics. At age four she accompanied her father to the Pacific Garden Mission in Chicago and stood up at testimony time to share the verse (but not the reference) "Twinkle, twinkle, little star / How I wonder what you are." It was greeted with resounding "amens." She later joined Bible Memory Association and learned many passages in the King James Version, citing chapter and verse before and after. Now a Spanish teacher, she and her husband, the son of an evangelical minister, live in Connecticut with their two born-again children.